SIGNPOSTS TO PERFECTION

TO MY MOTHER

SIGNPOSTS
TO
PERFECTION

A SELECTION FROM THE SERMONS
OF JOHANN TAULER

Selected, edited and translated
by
Elizabeth Strakosch

B HERDER BOOK CO
15 & 17 South Broadway
St Louis 2, Mo.

© 1958 by Blackfriars Publications

Nihil obstat : Carolus Davis, S.T.L.
Censor deputatus

Imprimatur : E. Morrogh Bernard
Vic. Gen.

Westmonasterii, die 29a Aprilis, 1958

Printed in Great Britain by Arthurs Press Ltd., Woodchester, Glos., and bound by Kemp Hall Bindery, Oxford.

CONTENTS

INTRODUCTION

1. *A man's world*

When history is presented to us through the medium of dates, names of places where battles were fought and the dynasties of rulers, it has a paralysing effect on our brain, because the imagination immediately conjures up the class-room in which we once sat, trying to memorise completely undigestible matter; the power of our productive imagination deserts us and the story of our ancestors and of mankind in general becomes as dry as the dust to which our forefathers have been reduced. When, however, we are confronted with the story of one particular man who lived centuries ago and when we are attracted by his personality, our interest is awakened, we want to know how he lived, what his political, social and personal circumstances were, which contributed to the making of the man we imagine he must have been.

Such a character was Johann Tauler. We know very little about him and can only attempt to reconstruct his character, as far as this is possible, by the sermons which have been handed down to us. These show that he must have been a man of great psychological insight and deep wisdom, yet of a childlike simplicity and directness in his relation to God. Although his comparisons, chosen from every-day life to illustrate the thoughts he wished to convey, are at times somewhat forced and his scientific statements, to say the least, a little inaccurate, and though he sometimes ascribes his quotations to the wrong prophet, these are only minor details which perhaps even round off the human picture his sermons evoke. Nor must we forget that his sermons, as handed down to us, were not written by him personally (it is assumed that only one of the few manuscripts which we possess was corrected by him) but by nuns who, while listening to him, made notes and wrote the sermons down afterwards. As those who have listened to a lecture on a difficult subject and tried to write it down in longhand will know, it is virtually impossible to record it word for word and at the same time take in its full implications, particularly when the lecture treats of subjects such as mysticism and deeply religious concepts. Invariably it becomes necessary to add a word here and there in order to give the notes the shape and character of proper sentences and it is inevitable that, in translation from the spoken to the written word, some misconceptions creep in. We also find that a number of words have been mis-spelt and the punctuation is such that at times the sentences go on interminably without so much as a comma, let alone a full stop. Moreover, words used at the time of Tauler have often completely changed their meaning in modern usage or, even worse, have become entirely extinct, so much so that we have no equivalent for them nor are we able to trace their precise meaning.

The year 1300—or 1301, the date is not quite certain—which witnessed the birth of one of the

most prominent preachers and mystics of all time
was by no means a peaceful one. Pope Boniface VIII,
that determined, stern and indomitable follower of
Christ, occupied the papal throne; Philip the Fair of
France, Edward III of England and Albert of
Austria who ruled Germany were continually at war
with one another except when they united in an
attempt to undermine the power and authority of
the Vicar of Christ. The following story is well
suited to illustrate Pope Boniface's character. French
forces under the leadership of William de Nogaret
had invaded the little town of Anagni, the Pope's
native town where he was staying at the time, and
with drawn swords they had forced their way into
the Pope's presence. Boniface, then a man of
eighty-seven years of age, confronted them, sitting
upon his throne attired in his pontifical vestments
and holding a crucifix in his hands. The majesty of
his person was such that one of the assailants shrank
back but Nogaret, son of a heretic and filled with
hatred against papal—or any other—authority,
shouted at the Pope, threatening to have him
carried off to Lyons as a prisoner. Boniface replied
calmly: 'Here is my head, here is my neck. I, a
Catholic, the lawful Pontiff and Vicar of Jesus
Christ on earth may patiently bear to be condemned
and deposed. I desire to die for the faith of Christ
and his Church.' After a short captivity of three
days he was rescued by the indignant inhabitants of
Anagni.

Tauler, as far as we know, came from a wealthy
and property-owning family and it is surmised that
he joined the Dominicans at a fairly tender age, first

for the sake of education and then so as to be received into the order. It is certain that he was living at the convent in Strasbourg during the years around 1314, when Meister Eckehart held the position of prior and we know that Tauler was deeply impressed by that master and during his whole life remained loyal to him and his teaching. The accusations made against Eckehart's teaching must have dismayed Tauler and caused him much grief, because he says in one of his sermons—though he does not mention Meister Eckehart by name— that 'a well-loved Master has written and preached to you about this mystic union with God, but you did not understand him. He spoke in terms of eternity and you interpreted his words in terms of time . . . That unique Master spoke to you of that rare perception which knows neither form nor way . . .' The shock of the condemnation, by a papal bull, of twenty-eight of Meister Eckehart's statements must have had a lasting effect, for one can notice a certain restraint in Tauler's sermons, as if he would not allow his spirit to soar to its highest peak whilst preaching. In one of his sermons he even refutes the accusations made against him, that he is supposed to have told people that he would refuse to hear their confession unless they did what he told them to do. 'It would be entirely wrong,' he remarks, 'to say: "do what I want you to do," because I want everybody to act according to the law and I do not expect anybody's promise on that issue'. There were obviously always some people only too ready to cast a shadow of doubt on those mystics who inspired and enlightened the people with their words about the relation of the soul to God and about man's inner life. If one reads between the lines one is even inclined to wonder whether Tauler's repeated references to 'worldly hearts under a clerical garb' are not his way of replying to the accusations of those secular priests who were not in favour of the Mendicant Orders—Dominicans and Franciscans in particular—who not only drew large crowds to their churches, but also often deprived them of the monies which—as the priests thought—were their due. Moreover, the Mendicant Orders—at least during the first phases of the Interdict which lasted for some years—made use of their privilege to celebrate Mass and distribute the Sacraments in spite of the ban imposed on the country and these activities perhaps increased the envy of the secular priests who, if they were loyal to the Pope, had to live in enforced idleness.

In 1316, after a span of more than two years during which the conclave of cardinals had not been able to agree on the choice of a pope, John XXII was elected Vicar of Christ. His predecessor on the papal throne, Clement V who, until his election as pope had been entrusted with the Archbishopric of Bordeaux and was of French ancestry, had decided, much against the cardinals' wishes, to remain in France for his crowning instead of receiving the papal tiara in Rome. Thus was the foundation laid to the popes' 'exile' in Avignon which was to last for seventy years and to end, thanks to the entreaties of another great Dominicaness, St Catherine of Siena. John XXII, himself of French extraction, also chose Avignon as his place of residence and the building of the papal palace was begun during his pontificate. It soon became apparent that the policy of the Popes while they resided in France would be influenced by French policy and the wars and strife in Germany during that particular period bear vivid testimony to that theory. Whilst Germany was divided amongst itself and its manifold princes and rulers, large and small, engaged in warfare against each other, France could thrive and strengthen its position inside and outside its boundaries. The conditions in Germany at that time were such that they gave France every reason for hope that their policy would meet with success.

After the death of King Henry VII this unhappy land was divided into two camps. Frederick of Austria and Louis of Bavaria, both grandsons of Rudolph of Habsburg and aspirants to the German throne were each crowned King of Germany on the same day, 25th November 1314, Frederick in Bonn and Louis in Aix-la-Chapelle. As the papal throne was vacant neither of the two elections could be confirmed by papal authority and Louis, taking advantage of that situation, decreed that the election of a German King was not subject to confirmation by the Pope. After years of enmity which divided the country into two hostile camps, Louis defeated Frederick in 1322 at the battle of Muhlheim, took him prisoner and proceeded to assume the title of King of the Romans. Pope John XXII, indignant at Louis's self-determined action in deciding by force of arms which of the elections was valid, commanded him to appear at the papal court to answer the charges laid against him. Louis, in an erstwhile

polite note, asked for an extension of time in which
he might be required to present himself, which was
granted, but he soon changed his tune and issued a
memorandum in which he accused the Pope of
having heretical sympathies; he also insisted in an
aggressive tone on his kingship, whereupon the
Pope, in 1324, excommunicated him and his empire.

Tauler was by then twenty-three years of age and,
one may suppose, a fully-fledged preacher. His
native town of Strasbourg was in the thick of the
battle, as its Archbishop stood loyally by the
Church's ruling and refused Louis his kingly
honours while in that city, whereas the population
and civic authorities were divided in their loyalties,
some for and some against the Pope. When, however,
some of the higher clergy took sides with Louis and
joined the anti-papal ranks, the confusion was
complete.

To add insult to injury Louis, after having
brought about a reconciliation with Frederick who
retired into Austria, proceeded, at the head of an
army, to Milan and there, accompanied by those
prelates who had declared themselves for him and
thereby incurred their excommunication, he let
himself be crowned King of Lombardy. Then he and
his army continued on their way to Rome where, in
1328, Louis received the crown of the Holy Roman
Empire from the hands of the soldier Sciarra
Colonna, the 'Captain of the people', whilst one of
the excommunicated prelates anointed him. But
when Louis, in the presence of the assembled people
of Rome, appointed a monk as anti-pope, accusing
the rightful Pope of heresy and breach of the peace

the cup was filled to overflowing and the proud
Romans, who deeply resented the absence of the
Popes from their city and took umbrage at Louis's
high-handed ways, gave vent to their pent-up fury,
causing Louis to make a somewhat hasty retreat,
harassed as he was by the news which had reached
him that the Romans intended to join hands with
Robert of Valois who was marching from Naples
towards Rome. Louis's return to Germany was by
no means that of a victorious Emperor, and seeing
the state into which he had plunged his country by
his headstrong and autocratic actions, he seems to
have deemed it expedient to crave pardon from the
Pope. Through the channels of his friends he
approached the Pope with a view to making a
reconciliation possible but the Pope, influenced
by his French advisers, made such harsh demands
that Louis could not see his way to accept them and
even when, in 1334, Pope John XXII died and
Pope Benedict XII followed him on the throne, the
repeated attempts at peace made by Louis did not
meet with success. Such was the enmity between
Pope and King, that Pope John XXII declared that
everyone who fought Louis would be granted the
same indulgences as if he had been on a crusade and
that all the clergy who stood by Louis would be
suspended. Louis, on his part, decided, when he
returned to Germany, that any priest who adhered
to the interdict and refused to distribute the
Sacraments, would be made prisoner.

Tauler, the loyal son of the Church, together with
his fellow-Dominican brethren, being forced by the
anti-papal authorities to leave Strasbourg in 1339,

went to live in Basle, where they remained until 1347 or 1348, preaching, teaching and fulfilling their priestly duties. Some Protestant authors have claimed that Tauler was also amongst the excommunicated priests and that this was the reason why he had to leave Strasbourg. Recent research, however, has established beyond doubt that at no time during his life or after was he or his sermons under the ban or declared to be of a heretical character. The error arose through the invention of the writer Daniel Specklin (died 1589) who related how Tauler is supposed to have declared that he would remain in Strasbourg and not desert the people who suffered innocently for the sins of their rulers. This story is a mere fabrication and comes under the same heading as the one by Rulman Merswin which relates how a layman had a vision during which he was told to go to a town a hundred leagues away where he would find a famous preacher; the layman, after hearing the preacher realised that, though he was very learned and a gifted speaker, his sermons did not spring from his heart which was full of conceit; but eventually the layman, guided by further visions, was able to convert the preacher. For centuries this story was believed to refer to Tauler and only H. S. Denifle, towards the end of the last century, proved that not only did the story not refer to Tauler, but also that it was a mere fairy-tale, written with the purpose of enhancing the reputation of the 'Gottesfreunde', the Friends of God. These Friends of God took their name from the passage of St John 15, 15: 'I will not now call you servants, for the servant knoweth not what his lord does. But I have called you friends, because all things whatsoever I have heard of my Father, I have made known to you.' They were honest God-seeking men and women, married and single, laymen, friars and nuns who, without being united into one single community, were bound together by the urge to live a spiritual rather than a worldly life, to help the poor and to attain as near a relation to God as possible. More than once Tauler refers to them and advises his hearers to seek the advice of these holy people; he says: 'For those who wish to live for the truth it would be very beneficial if they had a Friend of God to whom they could go for spiritual advice and who would direct them according to the Holy Ghost . . . and they should seek out an experienced Friend of God who can show them the right path, even if it meant walking as far as a hundred miles.' Whilst these Friends of God were under the leadership and spiritual advice of the clergy they performed many good deeds and many amongst them reached a high degree of sanctity. But after Tauler's death in 1361 and Suso's death in 1366 the movement soon deteriorated and it was not long before one of them, Nicolaus von Basel, was condemned as a heretic, thereby bringing the whole movement—or what was left of it in its original form—into disrepute.

Tauler, at the age of forty-three and in the prime of his life, was living in Basle when, in 1343, Pope Clement VI, successor to Benedict XII summoned Louis of Bavaria to come to the Papal Court in Avignon to make amends and restore peace. But once more the conditions were such that Louis refused to accept them, nor did he make another

attempt to seek forgiveness from the Pope, whereupon Clement ordered the German electors in 1346
to proclaim Charles of Luxembourg as their king,
thereby deposing Louis. Charles IV, however, the
'Pfaffenkönig' as he was called (*Pfaffe* being a
derogatory term for *priest*, i.e., the king appointed
by the clergy), did not conform to the rule insisted
upon by the Pope that the election of the king must
depend on the Papal confirmation. He only asked
the Pope for his grace and goodwill and not for
confirmation of the election. Soon afterwards, in
1347, Louis was killed in an accident whilst
hunting and though it was rumoured that he had
been murdered, no evidence of such a crime was
forthcoming and the country lived in the hope that
it might enjoy a period of peace and tranquility.

However, God ordained otherwise and in 1348
the Black Death broke out in Strasbourg. This
terrible plague, which in Strasbourg alone claimed
14,000 victims, brought untold misery wherever it
reared its ugly head and between the years 1348 and
1350 it appeared again and again in various parts of
Europe. While death stalked the streets of his native
town, Tauler returned from Basle to this unfortunate
city to take up his duties again.

And what of the women who were left behind for
months and years while their husbands were engaged
in warfare in far away lands? Even when the women
lived on farms and could grow enough food for their
daily sustenance, they had to care for and bring up
the children single-handed. When they belonged to
a higher grade of society they had to supervise the
work of the servants and of the people in their

employ, if the husband was in a trade that had to be carried on in his absence; in short, they had to take over a man's responsibilities and to maintain the normal way of life as best they could. We do not know much of the everyday woman of the Middle Ages, but we do know that she was brought up in the tradition that a woman's place is in her home, that her calling is to have and rear children and that, according to the Church's teaching, she should obey her husband and fulfil the sacrament of matrimony by standing by him and form—as it were—a steady background from which husband, children and servants could derive strength and steadfastness. One must not imagine that the medieval woman was of the meek-and-mild, mousy type, so familiar to us from the way women of the Victorian era were forced to appear. On the other hand she was not a masculine type, but retained her feminine character-istics, and at the same time often attained to a very high standard of learning. The fine qualities and noble minds of medieval womanhood have been immortalised in the songs of the Minnesingers, even if we allow for a certain amount of poetic licence in the songs dedicated to the minstrel's lady-loves.

The faith of the Middle Ages was still far more imbued with the knowledge of the unique position of the Virgin Mary in the divine plan for the redemption of mankind, of her quiet way of working tirelessly in the shadow of her divine Son, a willing tool without claim of reward. This veneration of our Lady must have had a lasting influence on the medieval attitude towards womanhood and only when the Reformation uprooted this devotion in the hearts of many, did the true position of woman begin to be misunderstood and her inheritance—steady and quiet dignity—was replaced by complete subjugation to the all-powerful male which eventually led to the struggle for emancipation and so-called equality. The consequence was and still is the complete loss of her original calling.

2. *A woman's world*

It is interesting to note that the institution of nuns' convents goes back to the era of the very early Christians and that women were the first to dedicate their lives to Jesus Christ without thoughts of missionary work but rather for the sole purpose of working for the Church, as true spouses of Christ the King. In fact, in the person of Mary Magdalen, of whom Jesus Christ said: 'Mary has chosen the best part,' we find the first Christian contemplative.

The wars and upheavals of the fourteenth century wrought havoc amongst the male population of Germany and the result was a surplus of women, some of whom were widowed and others who remained single. Those who wished to embrace the religious state had the choice of a variety of vocations. They could either be enclosed nuns in which case they were bound by profession and had to live according to the strict rules of their order. They were not allowed to go out but could teach a limited number of girls within the precincts of the convent. They could also take the vow of virginity and be solemnly consecrated by the bishop. If they wished to become canonesses they lived in a community

and took the vows of chastity and obedience.
There were congregations which worked as sacris-
tans, others cared for the sick and the poor, others
again for the lunatics. The Beguines, for instance,
famous throughout the Middle Ages, lived in a
community for a time and could then return to live
in the world; they took no vows, but kept as near as
possible to the Christian ideal of poverty, though
they did not beg for alms, but worked for their
living.

The nuns' convents were affiliated to the
monasteries of the same order and were not allowed
to have their own superior general. The laws relating
to the convents were extremely strict and an
institution like that of Mary Ward who, in the
seventeenth century, founded a teaching congregation whose members were only bound by simple
vows and who had their own superior general, was
suspended in its original form by the Holy See.
Mary Ward had given her foundation a constitution
after the model of the Society of Jesus—they were
also nicknamed the Jesuitesses—but after many
years of trials during which she journeyed in France,
Flanders, Italy and Austria, she reformed the
constitution in a way that was approved by the Holy
See. To this day the schools which she founded
flourish in Germany and Austria and the congregation is called 'Englisch Fräulein'.

The nuns proper who had chosen the contemplative way of life were enclosed in their convents
and lived according to the rules which the monks of
the same order observed in their monasteries. They
took the three vows of poverty, chastity and

obedience and followed the monastic observances which prescribed perpetual abstinence from the Feast of the Exaltation of the Cross on September 14th to Easter Sunday and on all Fridays throughout the year. The nuns were only allowed to use wool for their personal clothes as well as for their bed-clothes and they had to sleep on a hard bed, no single cells being permitted, only a common dormitory. The silence was almost perpetual, but the nuns had to assemble every so often in chapter and publicly acknowledge their faults and they were expected to perform a certain amount of penitential practices. They recited the canonical hours in choir and were engaged in every kind of manual labour necessary for the smooth running of the convent's household.

Many of these women came from high society, and though girls of the poor classes who could neither read nor write learned nothing except their catechism, and spent their lives minding the animals, the young ladies of the educated classes went through a course of extensive learning. The daughters of reigning princes, for instance, were placed in the care of a lady-teacher who taught them music and general behaviour, as well as spinning, weaving, cutting out and sewing their own and their husbands' clothes. It was a general rule that women not only knew how to bake their own bread, but were also able to brew the beer.

Monks were employed at these courts for the teaching of the scientific subjects and though, as for instance in English convents, the girls were also given a classical education, their knowledge of literature was generally restricted to the reading of

Holy Scripture and it was also the usual thing for a woman to read her Psalter day by day. Thus she was thoroughly acquainted with it and one need not be surprised to see how in many cases it influenced her whole attitude towards life. Convents in England seem to have had a particularly high standard of learning, so much so that St Lioba, a relation of St Boniface, after having been trained in such a college, followed St Boniface to Germany, where she founded a teaching convent near Wurzburg and trained German nuns for that profession. On the other hand we must not imagine that it was the general rule for men and women of that period to master the arts of reading and writing, all the more when we learn that a great poet like Wolfram von Eschenbach was not able to read or write.

Our materialistic age is inclined to look upon any men or women who embrace the religious state as people who either wish to evade the responsibilities which life seems to lay upon their shoulders or as people who flee the world because they have experienced a great disappointment. Neither of these motives will ever be instrumental in the making of a good religious, because they are merely of a negative character. The calling to and vocation for the religious state is a very positive one and although the horrors of worldly events may influence someone to take the veil or to become a monk, it is primarily the realisation of the need for powerful and concentrated prayer, to counteract the terrible evils of the world, which induces such people to enter a convent. It is certainly not the fear of the weakling who trembles at the thought of having to face the vicissitudes of life. And strange as it may sound to the ears of those who only accept as real value what they can take in with their five senses or of those who entirely reject God, it is nevertheless true that they are the dreamers whereas the God-seekers are the realists because, the more one attunes one's life to the truth, the nearer one is to its essence, the reality of God.

It is generally assumed that the terrible wars and upheavals of the thirteenth and fourteenth centuries were the indirect cause of the birth and blossoming of mysticism, but against that it must be argued that many dreadful tragedies have ravaged mankind and countries in the course of history without producing the revival of an intense religious life, let alone mysticism. So many coincidences of historical, social, religious and other factors had a hand in the making of this particular period that it seems futile to look for 'the reason why'; let us acknowledge that it happened in 'God's good time'. Also there were many thousands of holy men and women who were not mystics and Tauler refers to them time and time again in his sermons. Occasionally even a somewhat ironical note creeps into his addresses, when, for instance he says: 'But fear not, my honourable ladies! There are also those who drink and eat abundantly, yet they live devoutly and still arrive at the godly state, so that if you do not aim any higher, you still need not be afraid.' As he invariably addressed the nuns in his spiritual care as 'my dear children', he probably referred in this particular instance to the laity amongst the congregation and one can almost visualise the apprehensive expression

in the faces of the 'ladies' when he spoke at length
about God who tries, chastises and drives man until
'he abandons himself and all things he clings to
which hinder him on his way towards true perfection'.

As I have said, the nuns of the various orders were
affiliated and under the spiritual guidance of the
monasteries of the same order. The friars had to
satisfy the nuns' spiritual hunger, and preaching
was amongst their most important duties. One often
hears of sermons lasting for an hour or more and
amongst Tauler's sermons we sometimes find two
to three relating to the same feast-day. As he refers
in his second sermon to the first, one must assume
that both were delivered on the same day and not
collected from one year to another. Also they had to
be of a fairly high standard as the congregation
consisted of many educated women who followed
them closely and with deep interest. It is to these
women who took the immense trouble of writing
down the sermons they heard, that we owe a great
debt of gratitude, because it is due to them that
the deep thoughts and conceptions of mysticism
have been preserved and handed down to us. Names
like the visionary Benedictine nun Hildegard von
Bingen in the twelfth century, Mechtilde von
Magdeburg, Christine and Margarete Ebner and
Elsbeth Stagl who lived in Tauler's century, have
become a beacon and guide for women who combine
great knowledge with a saintly life.

Though the nuns to whom Tauler preached were
often well educated, they were nevertheless not
learned enough to have a thorough knowledge of

Latin, so that he could not have preached in that
language and consequently he and his contemporaries
like Meister Eckehart, Suso and other masters were
forced to speak in German. Many theological
concepts had hitherto never been expressed in the
vernacular and linguistic terms had to be found to
make the ideas comprehensible. An entirely new
vocabulary was needed for that purpose and the
German language with its peculiar gift of expressing
deeply philosophical and religious thoughts and
ideas is indebted to that particular period when,
from sheer necessity, its foundations were laid.
Great modern scholars are engaged in the study of
words and terms used by Tauler and his contemporaries which, as mentioned above, have either
changed their meaning in modern usage or have
altogether fallen into disuse. Words like *Gemuet*
which in modern German is more or less equivalent
to the English concept of sentiment—not sentiment-
ality—or frame of mind, seems to have been used
by Tauler as representing a notion far more related
to the will than to sentiment. The word *Angenommenheit*, when transcribed into modern language
could mean *taken upon oneself* or *accepted* and
actually when Tauler speaks of the *Angenommenheit*
of Jesus Christ he means his quality of being God
and Man, whereas when the word is used in
conjunction with human beings it conveys the
meaning of a habit, of a quality one has acquired.
The word *smacken* offers an interesting development.
It is fundamentally the same as the modern German
word *schmecken*, i.e., to taste. The person who tastes
or has taste takes in what he sees and knows what

he likes or, in other words, he can *discern*. In actual fact the translation which comes nearest to the middle-high-German term of *smacken* is to discern.

Tauler, as well as Eckehart, Suso and others use the word *Grund*, the ground of man's inner being. We may try to substitute modern terms like 'the core' or 'pith' of the soul, the 'marrow', the 'centre', and others, but we shall never arrive at the essence of the word as used by the mystics. It conveys the impression of something dark, obscure and indiscernible by the understanding and as a matter of fact the mystics use it to describe the abode in the human soul which cannot be discerned by the senses and which, if man gives himself to God, is inhabited by him. Incidentally, the word *Grund* forms part of the word *Abgrund*, or abyss, one of the characteristics of which is that it is unfathomable and dark. Tauler keeps on impressing on his hearers that they must clear the ground of their soul so that God can take up his abode and guide man's life and he compares God with the sun when he says: 'Although it (the sun) is at least six times the size of the earth, you can, by taking a basin full of water, putting a mirror at the bottom and placing the basin in the garden when, during summer-time, the sun stands in its zenith, see the whole disc of the sun reflected in the mirror as a small base. Yet, as soon as an obstacle, however small, gets in between the little mirror and the large sun, it immediately robs the mirror of the sun's reflection. It is exactly the same with man who has made an obstruction in his soul; however small it may be, he can no longer see the ground. There is no doubt that the obstacle robs him of the possibility of the supreme goodness—God himself—being reflected in his soul.'

The most controversial term used by the mystics is the word *nichts* or 'nothing' when applied to God. It does not mean, as some people might suspect, a negation of God's existence but the very opposite. The mystics try to convey the utter impossibility of expressing God and his attributes in human language. Whatever one says of him is imperfect because it only applies to one side of him, whereas he is everything, everywhere and all the time, or rather outside time. Tauler quotes one master as saying: 'Man conveys the loveliest things about God when, overwhelmed by the knowledge of his innermost riches, he keeps silent . . .' and 'one master praised God in words, but another master heard him and rebuked him, saying: "Be quiet, you are blaspheming".' Tauler comments that both masters were right.

He has very sensible advice to give the nuns under his spiritual care. He admonishes them that 'as a good wine must be kept in a good cask, so a wholesome body is the proper foundation for a well-appointed inner ground . . .'. He tells them that only those to whom nature has given a robust health need follow the strict rule and even with them he does not insist upon it. When they get tired and weary they should not force themselves to remain in an uncomfortable position because 'when the body is overworked . . . it takes its toll in various ways . . .' and the observation that 'a good meditation, even when it is interrupted by occasional nodding is much more beneficial than many outward exercises of the senses while one is wide awake' seems sound advice for nuns, who get up soon after midnight to attend their first Mass and should remain in church 'for the duration of a sung Mass', in order to meditate.

It seems that indignant voices were raised at some point during Tauler's life as a preacher, that the older nuns were too stern in enforcing the strict rule of the order, because he speaks about the sick mind of the young generation and of the great need they have of receiving Holy Communion as often as possible to improve their spiritual strength. He says: 'It is the sick who need the physician, not those who are in good health' and pleads with the young sisters that while they 'live in these troublesome times, your devotion should not slacken or, even worse, die out altogether. Human nature is not as steadfast as it was of old and unless we hold on to God with our whole strength we must needs succumb.'

But Tauler defends the older sisters who have been 'active and filled with sanctity at a time when humanity was not in such a sad plight as it is to-day and thus they were extremely severe in the execution of their order's rule'. When he says: 'Do you realise how many convents have been made to endure incredible suffering? Had it not been that they persevered as ardently with their wonderful devotions as had always been their wont, they would not have survived,' he is obviously thinking of convents which were attacked or destroyed by armies.

He could, however, also be a strict master, as when he reproaches the nuns for not keeping silence in the places where it is demanded and he insists that unless they keep silent they will not achieve that quietude and inner peace without which God cannot operate in their souls. Also he admonishes them to remain secluded before and after receiving Holy Communion, in order to prepare themselves for the Sacrament and to be ready to reap the benefit of it. 'It is a great pity,' he says, 'that you do not remain secluded in order to become aware of the benefit of the Food. At times it bears fruit on the third or even as late as on the fourth day if only you would watch and remain alone, but that is precisely what you refuse to do. The fruits of the Holy Sacrament cannot be born within you unless your mind is ready to receive them with love and you are withdrawn within yourselves.'

Thus it is that, although we have to thank women for preserving the precious sermons of men like Tauler, Meister Eckehart and Suso, it was they and others like them who delved unceasingly into the mysteries which surround us and who brought inner and outer experiences, images and conceptions into relationship with God. Whereas the women were gifted and willing pupils they needed the trained and deep searching minds of the men to supply them with the spiritual food for which they longed.

3. *A Mystic's world*

Except for the fact that Johann Tauler's tombstone records that he died in 1361, hardly anything is known about him after his return from Basle to Strasbourg in 1348. It is reasonable to presume that he remained in that city for the rest of his life apart from a few occasional visits to other places.

There is an interesting passage in his sermon for Ascension Day which must have been delivered when Tauler was in his fifties (he died in his sixtieth or sixty-first year). He speaks about the disciples who, after our Lord's Ascension, had to wait another ten days until the Holy Ghost came to comfort them and remain with them. Tauler elaborates on the theme that even the disciples, who had been in such close contact with our Lord and had been with him during the forty days between his Resurrection and his Ascension into Heaven, had to withdraw and remain in retreat, preparing themselves during ten days for the coming of the Holy Ghost. He compares the forty days, during which the disciples received our Lord's final instructions, 'opening their understanding' and telling them to 'stay in the city, till you be endued with power from on high' (Luke 24, 45 and 49) with the first forty years of our lives when 'man may do whatever he likes and may try as hard as he can, but he will never arrive at true peace nor be really godly until he reaches his fortieth year. Up to then he is troubled by many things, nature drives him hither and thither and is his master while he imagines that he is obeying God's commands . . . After that time he shall wait another ten years ere he is filled with the Holy Ghost, the Comforter, the Spirit who teaches all things.' He goes on to say: 'That is the moment when man should . . . sink down and be infused into the pure, divine and innermost truth, where life's noble spark is immersed in its original Power. If the return to that Source is truly accomplished, all sins are wiped out, even if their number had been legion and then all grace and bliss flows into man's soul. Then he really is a godly man, a pillar supporting the world and the holy Church.' These are not the words of a young man, but rather of one who has reached that blissful age, when the natural impulses have been conquered and the spirit is free to rise. Father Bede Jarret O.P., in his book, *No Abiding City*,[1] speaks about experiences in human lives and says (I quote from memory) that St Paul had not learned from books and other people's experiences how to strike a chord in every human heart, but by studying himself and applying that knowledge for the benefit of his fellow-men.

There is no evidence that Tauler acquired the title of Meister—as Meister Eckehart did—nor have any original manuscripts been found which prove that Tauler ever preached in Latin. He spoke and preached in his native tongue and did not tire of warning his hearers against the scribes amongst clergy and laity, the 'very clever people', as he calls them, who are 'the learned men who set great store by their knowledge . . . they are the reasoning people who judge everything by the rules of reason or the senses; taking in everything by the senses, their reason absorbs it and they make big words, glorying in them as if they understood great things. Their ground, however, from which truth should come forth, remains empty and deserted . . . Children, take no notice of them, for what nature gives, she claims back and what Christ gives, returns unto

[1]Blackfriars Publications 1956.

himself.' These words do not give the impression that they were spoken by a man very much in favour of book-wisdom and, in fact, Tauler almost repeats Eckehart's words when he says: 'The high clergy and great masters of the law debate about comprehension and love and which of the two is the more sublime. But we shall only deal with the Master of Life and if we succeed in that, we shall see the truth in all things.' There are also some people who are so convinced that they can solve every problem with the help of their reason that they drag down eternal truths—born in the spirit—to the level of their reasoning powers, so that they may 'understand it rationally and be able to expound it, thereby giving themselves airs and adding to their self-importance . . . They also view our Lord Jesus Christ's loving Image through the eyes of reason, but if they were to transfer their conception of it into the divine supernatural light they would soon see the difference and it would seem like the light of a candle as compared with the sunlight . . .'

Tauler's knowledge and understanding of the human mind must have been a source of great distress to the Devil, one of whose most ingenious tricks has been to convince mankind that he does not exist! Again and again Tauler, this physician of souls, drags the most secret and cunning devices of his adversary into the limelight, exposing them to the rays of his discerning wisdom. He explains how the Devil can use apparent sanctity for man's ruin, how he flatters him so that self-love and conceit make him perform good deeds in such a way that the world cannot but notice them. This sanctity,

emanating from delusion and the Devil, is expressed
somewhat blatantly in words and manners and the
enemy takes care that the delusion should continue.
'Such people are in rather a precarious position,
because the enemy so treats them that he may hold
them in (eternal) captivity. It would be better for
them if they ceased to pray because their kind of
prayer turns against themselves.' Tauler is most
insistent and keeps on repeating that anything we
cling to—be it representations, images, thoughts or
visions—is detrimental to our close union with God
because, if we do not dismiss them instantaneously
and return to the pure contemplation of him, they
become obstacles which hinder God from abiding
with us. When we hold on too long to 'sweet
raptures', trying to capture an intimate knowledge of
God's Presence, they are inclined to 'grow stale on
us', because the Devil is able to creep amongst our
closest relations with God and, by a touch of his
destructive hand, twist them and thereby blur our
mind so that, instead of being bare and open and able
to hear God's word, it is filled with the images and
representations which our senses have conjured up.
The reason for all this inability to hear and obey the
eternal Word is the Fall. 'Our first parents lent an
ear to the whisper of the enemy, which first deafened
them and then us, so that now we cannot hear nor
understand the adorable language of the eternal
Word . . . and mark my words, whatever it is that
attracts man inwardly or outwardly . . . the Devil
tampers with it, colours it with his taint and tempts
man with the faked object.'

Another of the Devil's artful devices is discussed

and thereby the sting robbed of its poison, when
Tauler speaks about the way in which man, when he
has succeeded in humbling himself, is immediately
assailed by the enemy who whispers in his ear:
'Now you are being humble, what a splendid
achievement!' Tauler says: 'Should a man discover
something in himself and take it to be humility
he is undoubtedly wrong' and he goes on: 'That is
why our Lord said: "Unless you become as little
children you cannot enter the Kingdom of Heaven".'
The lower, simpler and more direct we are in our
approach to God, the less chance we give to the
adversary to make us believe that we are ascending
the ladder of perfection whilst in fact we are
descending it rung by rung on our way to perdition.
'Deeply concealed in human nature lies a serpent,
feigning to be captivated by humility, yet in reality
lying in wait, ready to seize upon such spiritual
notions as can be grasped by reason and presenting
them in an earthly disguise, so that man, whenever
he succeeds in doing something, has the impression
that it was achieved by his own wit.'

Tauler seems to have had ample opportunity of
observing the damage done by malicious talk and
gossip. He tells the nuns in a very tactful way—as if
he were speaking in general—about people on
whom the Blessed Sacrament has little or no effect,
because they have some hidden fault which stands
in their way, and then he goes on to say: ' . . . it may
be an inward or an outward fault, it may even be that
they cannot guard their tongues' and while we can
almost see the twinkle in his eye when he says that,
he immediately implores the nuns not to give way to

this habit because 'there is no limit to the dreadful harm which arises from it'. At other times he is more explicit in his comment and compares the murderer who steals into our Lord's sheepfold with the person who kills his fellow-man's soul by passing judgement on him. 'It is the untold damage done by judging other people . . . which is often followed by a scornful attitude towards the other man's heart and inner self, but when it is expressed in bad manners and angry words it inflicts a fatal wound on the victim.' The evil, produced by the first man's malicious talk, spreads like a disease and poisons good and bad alike and Tauler's next words ring with indignation when he paraphrases the words of the gospel: 'Judge not that you may not be judged.' 'What do you know of your neighbour's inner ground?' he exclaims, 'how can you tell God's will with regard to him or in which particular way God has called or invited him? You dare take upon yourself to judge his works, you try to direct and rule him after your own ideas, thereby murdering God's will and inflicting your false verdict on your unfortunate neighbour!'

No wonder then, that Tauler instructed his nuns time and time again that unless they kept silence they would not come into close contact with God, because his word cannot be heard above the babel of voices, nor can God take up his abode in their souls if they are cluttered up with innumerable worldly interests. One must 'clear the ground', so that the soul which is 'a creation standing 'twixt time and eternity', always yearning for union with its Creator, may be able to receive him. Tauler remarks:

'When two things are to be united, the one must
suffer and the other must act. If, for instance, my eye
is to receive the impression of a picture on the wall,
it must eliminate all its own impressions or it will
not be able to reflect the picture, nor can the ear hear
one particular sound if it is filled with another kind
of noise. Whenever a thing is to receive something
it must be bare and empty.' When he speaks about
the soul being purified and re-formed by God he
says that it must discard its old self 'because whenever a thing is to be changed into something else,
it must first cease to be its old self; if wood is to
be changed into fire it must first lose the characteristics of wood. If you want to be absorbed into God
you must first shed your ego.'

As soon as the soul is bare and free from earthly
cares, the eternal Word comes and dwells in it;
inner peace, this most glorious gift we can offer to
God, is restored, and, supported by the knowledge
that God is within him, man can perform good
works. But as soon as he releases God's hand, as it
were, and disclaims his dependence on the divine
guidance his works, however good they may be,
sink down to the natural level where smugness and
pride lie in wait to overtake him. As long as one is
convinced of one's nothingness—God made man
from nothing—one is in direct communion with
the Maker, who steadies man and endows him with
the strength he needs to accomplish the works God
wants him to perform. In a sense the God-seeking
man is to be a sort of transmitting station between
God and the world. He should keep nothing for
himself, but pass on to his fellow-creatures what he

receives from God and offer to God the gratitude
he reaps from his fellow-men.

One must always bear in mind that preachers like
Tauler, Eckehart, Suso, Ruysbroeck and others
spoke primarily to enclosed nuns, and one cannot
help wondering whether the German mystics of the
fourteenth century sufficiently stressed the inter-
ceding aspect of a life devoted to God, instead of
regarding the temporal world as something implicitly
alien and evil; they searched ardently for an ever
closer union with God but did they endeavour to
plead for their fellowmen with the all-merciful
Creator?

Tauler's comparisons are usually of a more or less
robust nature, but he can also be very subtle. In one
of his sermons he elaborates on how a hard core
forms in the soul when man has committed a sin.
This core spreads imperceptibly like a skin,
becoming thicker in the same measure as one
continues in one's sinful ways. At last the soul is so
overgrown with it that neither God nor man can have
access to it. But when one pays attention to the hard
core when one first detects it, when one feels sorrow
because of one's sin and turns to God asking his
pardon, the aching hardness will instantly be
removed and the soul will be clear and rejoice in the
knowledge that once more it is accessible to God.
Tauler calls this examination of conscience the
inward confession, whereas the outward confession,
in his eyes, only restores the inner peace and calms
the gnawing conscience without having the healing
effect of the inward confession.

This director of nuns devotes one whole sermon

to the problem of how to make a good and short confession, because he maintains that many people make long confessions by merely repeating the same thing in different words, thereby wasting the priest's precious time and vexing and upsetting him. 'Believe me,' he says, 'you cannot rid yourselves of your sins by talking a lot about them . . . the outward repetition without inward communion bears little fruit.' But he also has very stern things to say about the scribes and pharisees amongst the people 'who are so clever that there is hardly one who goes to confession that is not full of tricks and dodges, whilst he clings all the time to his own views.'

When Tauler's sermons deal with human aspects of existence his words are earth-bound, homely and mildly insistent, but as soon as he speaks of divine conceptions, he cannot find sufficient words with which adequately to express his deep love and adoration for the Master. Tauler remarks more than once that human language is completely incapable of describing the sublime majesty of the all-loving God and once he exclaims: 'You don't know what real love feels like!' But *he* obviously knew and his voice, pleading with man that he should fill his life to the brim with burning love for his Creator, rings across the centuries.

The present volume consists of a selection of Johann Tauler's sermons, chosen from eighty-four sermons definitely ascribed to him and collected in a printed edition of 1498, a copy of which is kept in the North Library of the British Museum. I have also used Ferdinand Vetter's DIE PREDIGTEN JOHANN TAULER'S, Weidmann Berlin, 1910.

The sermons are arranged according to the ecclesi-
astical year. I wish to acknowledge my debt of deep
gratitude to the Reading Room and North Library
of the British Museum, and to the Institute of
Germanic Languages and Literature, University of
London, who, one and all, have most courteously
and generously put their libraries at my disposal, so
that I have been able to produce this book.

I have not attempted to write a theological
introduction, for the simple reason that I am not a
trained theologian. The only claim I can make in my
favour is that I know my own limitations. Scholars
in many lands are busy trying to throw further light
on the authorship of mediaeval manuscripts and no
doubt we can look forward to discoveries which will
reveal more facts and add colour to the canvas of life
as it was lived in the Middle Ages.

London W.2.   Elizabeth Strakosch.
June 19*th*, 1957.

SERMON FOR CHRISTMAS

This is the sermon on the threefold birth and it is taken from the three Masses on Christmas Day; it tells how we ought to gather our soul's three vital powers—memory, understanding and free will—and renounce all wilfulness, desires and mundane activities.

Holy Christendom celebrates this day the threefold birth, which ought to fill each man with so much joy and pleasure that he brims over in jubilation, love, gratitude and sheer delight. The man who cannot rejoice thus has every reason to be filled with fear.

The first and supreme birth consists in our heavenly Father begetting his only-begotten Son in divine substance, yet as a distinct Person. The second birth which we celebrate to-day is that of the child-bearing, brought about in virginal chastity and true purity. The third birth is effected when God, in truth and in spirit, daily and hourly is born in a good soul, bringing forth grace and love.

These three kinds of birth are celebrated to-day in three Masses. The first Mass is sung in the dark of the night and begins thus: *Dominus dixit ad me*. The Lord hath said to me, thou art my Son, to-day (meaning eternity) have I begotten thee. This Mass represents the hidden birth, brought about in the dark mystery of the fathomless Godhead.

The second Mass begins with the words: *Lux fulgebit hodie super nos*. A light shall shine upon us this day. It signifies the splendour of human nature

I

made divine and is begun in the night and concluded at dawn; for the birth took place unbeknown to many, yet known to some.

The third Mass is sung in broad daylight and begins thus: *Puer natus est nobis, et filius datus est nobis.* A Child is born unto us and a Son is given to us. It illustrates the loving birth which should and does come about every day and every moment in each good and holy soul when it turns to God with understanding and with love. For, if this birth is to become real and conscious, the soul must direct its entire strength into communion with God who will then become so much her own and give himself so utterly that never was anything known to be so complete. It is said that a Child is born unto us and a Son given to us. He is ours, entirely and above all ours, for all time and without intermission is he born in us.

We shall first deal with the birth of love of which this last Mass speaks, and how we can succeed in making this noble birth bear rich fruit in us. Consider then the first—the paternal—birth, when the heavenly Father begets his Son in eternity, because he will not keep to himself the abundant wealth of his goodness, but rather will share and let it flow in unlimited profusion. Both Boethius and St Augustine declare: 'It is part of God's very nature and character that he should give of his bounty; thus the Father, in begetting the divine Persons pours forth his goodness, infusing his creatures with it.' St Augustine also writes: 'We are good because God is good; all goodness in creatures comes only from God's essential goodness.'

Which then is the attribute of the paternal birth,

which we ought to observe and make our aim? To answer this question we must first understand the following truth. The Father as a Person in divine conception, turns his gaze upon himself, his clear perception penetrating the dark recesses of his eternal Being. He utters this supreme cognition of himself and the Word becomes his Son, born in eternity. Whereas when God rests within himself, he is essential Oneness, when he goes forth he does it as a distinct Person, God the Father. By concentrating and knowing himself, he brings the perception into being, the thought begetting the Word, conceived and affirmed as the second distinct Person, God the Son. Whereupon once more he reflects; seeing his perfect goodness and delighting in it, he pours forth his inexpressible love into the Holy Ghost, divine Love feeding and being fed by the eternal Source. In this way all that goes forth returns to its origin and that is the reason that Heaven's course is most noble and perfect; it truly returns whence it began. In the same way man's course is noble and perfect, for he too returns to his Source.

Our heavenly Father's withdrawing within himself and again going forth should also be practised by every man who wishes to become the fertile ground in which the divine birth can take effect; he too must withdraw within himself and then come forward again. But how can this be done? The soul possesses three noble powers—memory, understanding and free-will—which makes her a true image of Holy Trinity. These powers enable her to respond and grasp God, receiving all he is, has and is willing to give, thereby gazing into eternity; for the soul is a creation standing between time and infinity. With its supernatural part it stands in eternity, whereas its natural part is bound up with time and the animal forces.

But owing to Adam's fall and his association with the dark powers, the soul's superior as well as her inferior forces have been caught up in time and finite things; original sin has made light of this confusion and the soul is ready to spend itself in worldly things, thereby losing sight of eternity. Hence, if a loving birth is to take place, it is imperative that this worldly course should be reversed; that with all its strength the soul should hold communion with itself, collect itself and rally all interior powers, be they of the superior or of the inferior rank, calling to order all distractions; for forces are only strong when united. When a marksman wishes to hit his target he closes one eye, so that the other one may see all the better; in the same manner, if a man wishes to get to the bottom of a problem, he must concentrate on it, forcing all matters he deems important to unite in the soul, from whence they came, just as all branches grow from the tree-trunk. Once all these forces of the senses and the emotions have been raised to the highest level, their source, the communion, has been accomplished. Then man shall—as it were—step away and above himself, denying all his habits of will, desire and mundane activity. Only God's pure will shall be of importance, all self-interest and selfish aims be abandoned; he shall only exist for God, in order to obey him in things high and low, so that he may fulfil his work in the soul and bring about the birth, unhampered by the creature. When two things are to unite, the one must suffer and the other must act. If, for instance, my eye is to receive the impression of a picture on the wall, it must eliminate all its own impressions or it will not be able to reflect the picture; nor can the ear hear one particular sound if it is filled with another kind of noise. Whenever a thing is to receive something it must be bare and empty. St Augustine expressed it thus: 'Pour out, that you may be filled. Go out that you may enter.' Another time he exclaimed: 'Oh noble soul and creature why will you persist in going out in search of him, who all the time and in truth is in you, through whom you partake of the divine nature! Why then be concerned and troubled about other creatures?' When, however, man has cleared the ground and prepared the dwelling-place, it is beyond doubt that God must come and fill it; the heavens would sooner be rent asunder than that God would leave a soul empty. It would be against his nature, his essence and his justice. That is why you ought to keep in a state of quietude so that the Word of this birth may speak within you and be heard, for as soon as you speak he must fall silent. One cannot serve the Word better than by keeping still and listening. There is no doubt that as much room as you leave by stepping aside, will be taken up by him, no more and no less, and the egress will equal the ingress.

We find an illustration of this egress in the book of Moses, where it is related how God commanded Abraham to leave his country and his kith and kin, because he wished to give him all good things. They were nothing else but the divine birth, the supreme wealth. The land he was to abandon was his body with its lusts and disorders as we all experience them.

The friends he was to leave behind were none else than the inclinations of the natural forces in their various forms which made a slave of him, dragging him down. They also made him subject to love and grief, joy and sorrow, desire and fear, care and negligence. Mark my words, these friends are part of our very nature but if this real goodness, the true birth is to be effected in us we must completely exclude all else.

There is a saying that a child which has been spoiled at home behaves like a bully when amongst strangers. This is true insofar as human beings, who have never risen above nature and their sensory perceptions like seeing, hearing, tasting and feeling, who have never been outside the realm of natural things, are truly like so many bulls, when it comes to understanding these deeply divine matters. Their inner life is like an iron fortress into which no light can penetrate. When deprived of the use of their senses, of images and forms they can no more know or feel anything, because they have never overcome their natural self and therefore cannot embrace this noble birth. Of these Christ said: 'There is no man that hath left house or brethren or sisters or father or mother or children or lands for my sake and for the gospel, who shall not receive a hundred times as much.'

Until now we have spoken of the first and of the last birth, how the first should teach us how to understand the last one. Now in the light of the second birth we shall show that the Son of God was born this night of the Mother and became our Brother. He was born in eternity, a Son without mother and was born in time without a father. St

Augustine wrote: 'God's spiritual birth in Mary's soul made her far more blessed than his actual birth from her womb.' Whosoever wishes that this spiritual birth should take place in his soul must make Mary's qualities his own. She was a mother, both bodily and spiritually, a pure virgin though betrothed, and was withdrawn utterly secluded from all outward things when the Angel came to visit her. Such should be the state of a spiritual mother of God. She ought to be pure; even if she has been led astray by the world she can now turn back and become pure and chaste once more, for though virginity is outwardly barren, yet inwardly it bears rich fruit. This virgin should close her senses to the world and not strive after activity, because it would avail nothing. Mary, also, pondered over heavenly thoughts alone. Inwardly she should be productive, for the true glory of the eternal King's daughter shines only in her soul. If, in this way, the maiden excludes all her habits, manners, conduct and speech, steadying her mind on the one aim, then God, his Son and his Word, who embrace all things, will bear rich and great fruit in the fertile ground of her soul.

Mary was an espoused virgin and so should this maiden be, St Paul says that you should submerge your inconstant will in God's immutable will, so that he can help your frailty. Furthermore, Mary was in retreat and this bride of God should do likewise if she wants to establish the true birth in her soul. But the retreat should not merely be made because the time is opportune—this might prove to be of little value—it should also be made the occasion for a conscious practice of virtue and ought to produce a tranquillity in which the soul can hide from nature and the senses, reposing in inner peace and silence. The beginning of next Sunday's Mass speaks of this stillness. 'While all things were in quiet silence and the night was in the midst of her course, thy almighty Word leapt down from heaven from thy royal throne' (Wisdom, 18, 14); and the eternal Word proceeded from the Father's heart. This stillness, when all things rest in deep eternal silence, will help the Word to be truly heard; if God is to speak you must be silent and if God is to enter, all other things must be excluded. When our Lord entered Egypt, all the idols in the country fell. Your idols consist in all things, however good or holy they may seem, which lead you away from the true, immediate embrace of the eternal birth. Our dear Lord Jesus said: 'I came not to send peace, but the sword, to set a man at variance against his father and the daughter against her mother . . . ' Your great enemy is the unknown, for the variety of images which it conjures up conceals the Word and hinders its birth in you. Although these images do not altogether interfere with this quiescence, which in any case will sometimes desert you, a spiritual mother ought to concentrate on this birth and on tranquillity, thereby raising the practice to a habit; what seems an easy task to a trained mind will appear to be a great trial to an untrained mind; art must be practised. May God help us to produce that stillness in us which is essential for the noble birth, that we may become true spiritual mothers. Amen.

SERMON FOR THE VIGIL OF EPIPHANY

'Take the Child and his mother and go into the land of Israel.'
(Matth. 2, 20.) The sermon from St Matthew's gospel preached on the
eve of the twelfth day, treating of St Joseph's fears with regard to
Archelaus. It teaches how we should carefully consider every action
before embarking on it: we are also warned of three adverse forces
which endanger our soul.

If one were to read, preach and meditate on holy
Scripture over and over again, one would find every
time some new truth, hitherto undetected by men.

'Take the Child and his mother and go into the
land of Israel; for they are dead who sought the life
of the Child.' Dear children, there are many people
amongst us who, as soon as a new plan forms in their
mind and they take it to be a good one, immediately
want to put it into practice; in their first enthusiasm
over the inspiration they are so eager to rush into
action that they do not consider whether they will
be able to accomplish it, and whether they have
enough inner strength and grace to conclude the
noble work they began. That is why, before we
embark on a work, be it an outward or an inward
one, we must consider carefully whether or not we
can carry it through. As soon as we have reached a
decision we should turn our whole mind to God,
pleading with him that he may do his work in and
through us. Amongst those enthusiastic people
there are also some who soon abandon their first
plans; they start on new ones, with their minds

9

fluttering hither and thither. This irresolute behaviour often leads to the physical and mental ruin
of many a man, because he pursues his plans only
according to his own devices, his intelligence
usurping the place where God ought to reign.

St Joseph, having fled into Egypt with the Child
and his mother and later having been told in his
sleep by the Angel that Herod was dead, heard it
said that Archelaus who had succeeded his father as
ruler of the country would also try to kill the Child
Jesus.

How are we to interpret this passage? There is no
doubt that Herod, who persecuted the Child,
wanting to kill him, represents the world, which
kills the child in every man; if we want to keep the
child alive we must escape the world. When the
child—the soul—has withdrawn from the world,
perhaps even into a monastery or convent, Archelaus
rises up and claims his rulership. This tyrant is none
other than the agent for the entire natural world
which rises in rebellion within you and which you
will only conquer by a great deal of exercise and
perseverance and by imploring God's help; also you
must realise that you have many fierce enemies in
your breast who are always watching, ready to strike.

The first of these enemies is the world with its
spiritual pride, which whispers to you that you
want to be seen, respected by your fellow-men and
raised in their esteem. Consequently you want to
please the world by your attire, your conduct, by
resounding words, your way of life, your wisdom,
friends, influence, fortune and honour. These
companions, however, march under the Devil's
banner.

The second enemy is your own flesh which attacks you with the weapons of bodily and spiritual impurity, in words and in deeds. All these sins must be laid at the door of such people who misuse their pleasures, turning them into physical passion or a different kind of lust. Each man should observe carefully which of his senses is most vulnerable and most easily accessible to attacks of impurity. Wherever man's inner being is obsessed with love for created things, be they of the material or of the mental order, which force his will and his heart to concentrate on them by day and night, this man is guilty of having given way to the sin of impurity.

In the same way that physical unchastity soils the purity of the body, spiritual incontinence perverts the immaculateness of the mind and in the same proportion as the spirit is of a higher order than the flesh, this last sin does more harm than the first.

The third enemy is your hardness of heart, which makes you prone to the evil spirit's attacks of bitter and wicked thoughts when you are filled with suspicion, hatred and revenge and when you remember how someone has done you harm or spoken unkindly to you; then you are determined not to tolerate the insult, you scowl at him, threatening this fellow-creature of yours with angry words, trying to justify your ill-behaviour by being offensive. All this, undoubtedly, is instigated by the Devil.

Therefore, if you want to lead a blessed life you must flee from all temptations, because they truly represent the hard-hearted Archelaus. Fear for yourselves and the child within you, for he will certainly try to kill it. That is why St Joseph was anxious to find out whether there was anybody who sought the life of the holy Child. At the same time take heed that though you have overcome these initial vices, there are still a thousand chains which you must break and which are only known to those souls who have truly retreated within themselves. St Joseph, above all, stands for unwavering steadfastness in a divinely blessed life and steady progress in doing only God's will. He, forsooth, is the best guardian for the Child and his mother.

The angel warned Joseph and bade him return to Israel, which land stands for the state of contemplation. Many a man with an inclination for a holy life is misled at this stage by forcibly trying to free himself from his many shackles before God has delivered him from them and before the angel leads him away from himself and urges him on his way. This road leads to terrible pitfalls. Such people, helped only by their own wits, want to loosen their chains ere God loosens them; their ambition is to use big words and boasting of how they contemplated holy Trinity and other deep truths. It is deplorable to see the misery and delusions which have arisen and still arise every day from the refusal to bear with the shackles of the prison in the darkness of Egypt —for that land signifies darkness—although these people know full well that no earthly power can help or deliver them. Only God himself can achieve this. Even if you search and rush across the whole world, no one but God can offer you solace. He may choose to use some instrument to do his work—be it an angel or a human being—but nevertheless he and none other must perform the deed. That is why you should look for deliverance in your inner being, abstaining from forcible outward movement, and suffer yourself to be left in Egyptian darkness until the angel releases you.

St Joseph was warned while he slept. A man does not sin in his sleep—even if at times evil notions assail him—unless he, by his wicked deeds in his waking hours caused the thoughts to return in his sleep. We ought to appear to the outer world as if in deep slumber, passive to all suffering and temptations which may befall us, doing everything with calm and endurance, humbling ourselves, being inert as one asleep and untroubled; be still, and suffer to the end; there is no better way of freeing yourselves. Remain free of sin and you will be delivered in your sleep—the true inactivity—as St Joseph was delivered.

The prelates, priests and bishops, abbots, priors and prioresses of the Church should be guardians as was St Joseph. Every confessor should protect the young under his care and every man should treat his subordinates in a way profitable to them. We have many guardians and many masters. I, for instance, have a prior, a provincial, a master, a pope and a bishop who are all above me. If they were to wish me ill and became like so many wolves wanting to tear me to pieces, I would submit and suffer it with true meekness. Were they to wish me well and be good to me, I would accept it, but, I repeat, if they wanted to attack me, however many there were, I would suffer it and surrender.

St Joseph was filled with fear until the angel assured him that they were dead who sought to destroy the Child; only then did he seek to find out who had been appointed ruler of the country. People are wrong when they imagine that they must lose all fear. As long as we are in this world, we ought never to overcome this fear. *Timor sanctus permanet in saeculum saeculi:* holy fear shall be with us until the end of time. Even when the angel reassures you, do not give up fear, but search diligently for the ruler in your soul and see whether Archelaus is still the master.

St Joseph took the Child and his mother back to Israel. In the Child we recognise unalloyed purity; we should not get involved in things which do not concern us, but remain small, in lowly meekness. When we think of the mother, we are reminded of true love of God; love is the mother of deep humility and self-effacement which submits with a pure heart to God's will. At this early stage of our spiritual life we should not be free to go alone into the land of contemplation and even if we go there for a brief respite, we should then return to Egypt. It is certain that we ought not to remain in Israel before we have risen to full stature and have been found worthy of carrying the banner of our Lord Jesus Christ. After all, he taught us all things by his life so that, even if we could not hear the word of God, we could still take our example from the life of Jesus Christ. He came to Jerusalem when he was twelve years of age, but, not being fully grown, he left again and did not return until he was in his manhood. Then, when he was thirty years old, he came to Jerusalem every day, rebuking and correcting the Jews and showing them in masterly language where they had deviated from the truth. Preaching and teaching he remained in the country, free and subject to no one; coming and going as he pleased and being the Master, he brought about signs and wonders in Capharnaum,

Galilee and Nazareth, and in all parts of the land of Juda.

This is how man ought to live. He should not settle down in the land of contemplation, trying to live an exalted life, but should enter it and leave it again as long as he is not fully grown, but young and immature. When, however, he has arrived at maturity and is a man, he should go into the land of Juda, which represents the confession of faith to God. Then he may preach and teach in Jerusalem, the city of peace, and may also cross into Galilee. Thus he will be translated above all things, going to Nazareth, the true blossom from which spring the flowers of eternal life. Here he will find the real, assured foretaste or eternal life, complete certainty, inexpressible peace, joy and rest. Only those enter the land who yield, suffer and submit, who do not try to free themselves by force, but wait until God leads them on. They arrive at this peace in the full bloom of Nazareth and find there what they will enjoy in eternity.

May the loving God help us to partake of this peace.   Amen.

SERMON FOR THE FEAST OF EPIPHANY

This sermon, taken from the Epistle of Isaias, tells us in what way man should rise above himself and his fellow-creatures, so that God finds the ground prepared and can proceed with his work. 'Arise, be enlightened, oh Jerusalem.' (Isaias 60, 1.)

God longs for and is in need of one thing only in the whole world, and so greatly does he need it that he does his utmost to obtain it. It is simply this: he wants to find that the rich ground with which he equipped the noble human mind, is cleared and ready so that he can begin his divine work in it. For God, though all-powerful in heaven and on earth, is unable to do his most blessed work in man, without his creature's consent.

What contribution, then, can man make that God may let his light shine on this fruitful soil and perform his work? He should arise; *Surge*, says the Word (that is: arise). This evidently means that he should act. He must leave and go beyond himself and all creatures and everything that is not God. The result of this is an ardent longing; a great gust of wind, levelling all roughness, sweeps the ground and the stronger the reaction and the longer the duration, the greater will the longing become and the higher will it rise above itself, so that the mere touch of the cleared ground will at times stir the very depths of man's being.

Two different kinds of people react in two

different ways to this touch. The first kind, when they experience it, come to meet it with their natural alacrity, with great ideas and pictures conjured up by reason, thereby blurring the clarity of the ground. They still their longing by trying to listen to and understand the voice of reason which lures them into self-satisfaction and deceives them, making them believe that they are a Jerusalem—city of peace— while all the time they are only doing what is dictated by reason; alas, they think they have found inner peace. Others again, wanting to live by their own rules, devised in prayer or meditation, or resulting from the attempt to do what they see others do, try to do their own preparing of the ground and thus achieve inner peace; then they presume that they have truly become a Jerusalem, and are well satisfied with their works and ways and only content to follow the rules of their own making. It can easily be proved, however, that this peace is a fallacy. They still persist in their faults such as pride, carnal lust, satisfaction of the senses, subservience to other creatures and malicious judgement of people. As soon as they experience some vexation they retaliate in an undignified manner; their answer rings with angry words, expressed in hatred and ill-humour, because their wilfulness has been prevented from eradicating these various vices. Evidently they wish to till their own ground and God cannot work in it; their peace is a deception and they have not truly risen. These people should not imagine that they are a Jerusalem, nor should they boast of having the true peace; they must make a much greater effort to conquer their faults, taking our Lord Jesus Christ as their model in works of love and humility, thereby dying to themselves and learning how to rise.

The third kind, however, are the noble people. Rising in truth, they are inspired; they let God till their ground, giving themselves entirely to him, abandoning everything that is their own and saving nothing for themselves, neither works nor habits, action or repose, joy or grief. They accept all things from God in humble fear, offering them up again and keeping back nothing, in tranquillity and gentleness humbly bowing to the will of God. They are satisfied with whatever God decrees, be it peace or strife, for their own pleasure is God's good, well-pleasing will. Such people remind us of our Lord's reply, when his disciples urged him to attend the feast: 'My time is not yet come, but your time is always ready.' People such as these are always ready to suffer and to give way, but his time is not their time. Calm and long-suffering in patience they leave it to his divine will to choose the moment when he wants to work and inspire them.

They differ from the first kind inasmuch as they let God till their ground, not attempting to do it themselves although they, too, are subject to impulses and temptations of which none of us are free. But when they are brought face to face with these imperfections, be they pride or carnal desires, pleasure in temporal things, anger or hatred or whatever these vices may be which attack and greatly trouble them, they humbly approach God, asking him to deliver them from their temptations; they suffer his will to prevail and by this means literally rise above their own desires, thus coming to be a true Jerusalem, at peace in strife and joyful in sorrow. They rejoice in God's will so that the world cannot rob them of their inner peace and even if all the devils and all mankind had pledged themselves to uproot their peace of mind, they would not succeed.

God alone and no one else can satisfy people like these who are enlightened in the true sense of the word, for God sheds his all-pervading and pure light into their souls and his truth penetrates the deepest darkness and eclipses the brightest light. Indeed these are lovable and supernaturally godly people; none of their works is done without God and I think I can safely say that somehow they are not at all, but God is in them. They are excellent and worthy, carrying and supporting the world like steadfast pillars. How blessed and beautiful it would be, if one could but stand as firmly in righteousness !

The difference, then, between these two kinds of people is that the powers of the first kind—those who wish to till their own ground and will not submit to God to accomplish the work—are held captive by their faults and, not being able to rise above them they are in fact quite content to indulge in them and hold on to their self-will with pleasure. The second kind, however, the noble, blessed and calm people who submit themselves to God's will, rise above their natural selves so that, as soon as their failings beset them, they perceive and bring them to God, thereby destroying them. These, then, are the men and women firmly established in divine freedom. Can you wonder that they ask God to work their ground?

It is not seemly nor is it necessary that they should seek outward works. But what of the word *Surge*

which urges them to rise? Surely that means action?
Yes, certainly, there is one thing which they should
perform continually as long as they live and without
which man can never attain perfection; they must
always rise higher, lifting up their minds to God,
thus freeing their own ground and ask: 'Where is
he, who was born?' This question should be asked
in humble fear, inwardly watching for God's will
and fulfilling it. Should God send them suffering,
they will bear it, should he want them to act, they
will do so and should he send them understanding
and joy, they will accept it gladly. Their inner
ground bears witness that God has tilled and
purified it; he wants to be in sole possession of it and
nothing earthly is ever to trespass there.

God does indeed work in the ground of the first
kind of people, but indirectly, whereas he works
directly in the ground of the blessed people. But
nobody is able to express in words the works
accomplished in the ground directly touched by God,
nor can any human being communicate this
experience; it can only be known if it has taken
place in one's own soul but even then it cannot be
told.

When God has truly taken charge of the ground,
man loses all interest in outward things, whilst the
inward perception of God increases greatly. Should
a man achieve the highest point, which is only
reached by great perseverance and abundant grace,
he should abnegate himself completely, and thus,
however perfect he may be, he should always be
filled with humble fear and even when he has
reached the highest peak he should still think and
say: *Fiat voluntas tua*, 'Thy will be done.' He should

also consider carefully whether he is not in any way too attached to some outward things and whether God may not find something in his ground which could hinder him in the accomplishment of his noble and infused work.

May God's favour help us to raise ourselves in this way, so that he can do his redeeming work in us. Amen.

SERMON FOR THE SUNDAY BEFORE SEPTUAGESIMA SUNDAY

This sermon, taken from St Matthew's Gospel and preached on the Sunday before Septuagesima Sunday, tells how the soul hovers between time and eternity and how, if it detaches itself from all visual impressions, it carries a sweet yoke whilst the outward man bears a light burden. (Matth. 11, 25-30.)

Our Lord Jesus Christ, eternal Truth, said: 'My yoke is sweet and my burden light.' All those people who merely live an animal life contradict this statement by crying out that God's yoke is bitter and his burden heavy; yet the saying must be right since the eternal Truth pronounced it.

A yoke is something which you drag with great effort. When a thing weighs heavily and causes great hardship it is called a burden. The yoke applies to the inward man, whereas the burden stands for the outward, the old and merely natural man. The inner man, who comes from the noble regions of the divine and is shaped after the pure and supreme God, is always made welcome in his heavenly Father's house and longs for a return in order to partake of God's goodness. He can obtain by grace what is God's noble and blessed nature. He who could know and contemplate how God establishes himself in the ground of the soul, lying there shrouded and concealed, would indeed be blessed. Although man has turned away his eyes from God and has gone astray, he still feels an eternal calling and yearning for him; however hard man tries to escape from it, he can find no peace because nothing except the one aim can fully satisfy him. It drives and draws him unconsciously into his innermost being. The soul longs for its rest in God in the same way as all material things eventually come to rest in their appropriate places: the stone on the ground and the fire in the air.

Who, then, feels the sweetness of this dragging, heavy yoke? It is only sweet for those who have turned their eyes, their minds and their works away from the world. The soul hovers, as it were, between time and eternity; if it becomes involved in time it loses sight of eternity, but as soon as temporal things recede into a certain distance, they begin to appear small to the soul, as everything far away seems small whereas things nearby loom large because there is nothing to obscure the view. Take, for instance, the sun. Although it is at least six times the size of the earth you can, by taking a basin full of water, putting a mirror at the bottom and placing the basin in the garden when, during summer the sun stands in its zenith, see that the whole disc of the sun is reflected in the mirror as a small base. Yet, as soon as an obstacle, however small, gets in between the little mirror and the large sun, it immediately robs the mirror of the sun's reflection. It is exactly the same with man who has made an obstruction in his soul; however small it may be, he can no longer see the ground. There is no doubt that the obstacle robs him and prevents the supreme goodness—God himself—from being reflected in his soul.

Hence, however pure and noble the visual impressions may be, they still form an obstacle for the perfect vision, God himself. If the soul wants to reflect the Sun, it must be bare and free from all other impressions, because even one will obstruct the reflection. All those who do not try to achieve this bareness in order to clear the hidden ground, thus making it receptive, are of the purely material order and complain that the yoke is a bitter one. According to Origen, someone who has never seen or been conscious of this ground will never taste the joy of it.

No man lives the life of a true Christian unless he turns at least once a day—providing that circumstances permit—towards this ground. Those, however, who concentrate on this habit and are at their ease, eliminating all other impressions, so that the sun may pour into their soul, are convinced that God's yoke is sweeter than anything they have tasted—even sweeter than honey—and they consider everything else distasteful and bitter; in fact, all who have tasted the sweetness think that the world is as bitter as gall. This noble ground, once it is known to man, urges him on and draws him so vehemently, that it is as if his bones were emptied of their marrow and his veins drained of their blood. Wherever this true picture has taken shape, the effect of all harmful impressions is extinguished.

Visual impressions, whatever they may be, only hinder you because there is the danger that they may blur your true self. If you were to rid yourself of them and their characteristics, though you possessed a kingdom, it could do you no harm. Free yourself of pictures and their influences, but use all things as you need them. One holy man is said to have been so free of visual impressions, that none of them would remain with him. One day a man knocked at his door and asked for something; the holy man said he would go and get it. When he returned he had forgotten what it was. The other man knocked again and the holy man asked: 'What do you want?' Again he asked for the same thing and the holy man replied that he would fetch it; again he returned empty-handed. When the man knocked the third time, the holy man said: 'Come and get it yourself, I cannot hold on to pictures for so long, because my mind is now so free of them.'

God's sun shines into the free minds of these people and they improve by watching themselves and others, having given themselves and all things up to the divine will, wherein they are caught up. The imposition of God's yoke on them is so filled with bliss, that everything else is forgotten because it seems so small. They are approaching the eternal things, which appear large within their souls, because they are now so near and immediate. Such are the means by which people arrive at the sweetness.

Let us now consider the other sentence: 'My burden is light.' This refers to the outward man who is stricken with many sufferings.

Oh, merciful God, where can we find lovable people who consider that God's burden is light? Nobody wants to suffer, yet there must always be suffering and surrender, whichever way you turn. 'Christ had to suffer, in order to enter into his glory.'

In what way, then, should you suffer? In accepting God's judgement and decree, where or how they may befall you, be they sent directly from

God or through the medium of your fellow-men. If your friends die, if you are deprived of your fortune or your honour, of inward comfort from God or of outward comfort from creatures—carry these burdens lightly, in the same manner as you bear up with your own frailties, for which you are sorry but which you cannot overcome; lie down under the burden, suffering the divine will to be done and let God deal with it. The horse must draw the dungcart to the field, where its own dung from the stable, dirty and smelly as it is, produces the lovely wheat and the sweet wine, both of which would never grow, were it not for the manure. Remaining calm within yourselves, you, too, should with much trouble and care carry your uncleanness, your frailties which you can neither dispose of nor overcome, to the field of God's loving will and spread it on that noble field when no doubt a blessed fruit will grow from the soil of humble tranquillity.

Is there a man who, whether living in the land of plenty or in poverty, could bow under this burden, suffering God's will, judgements and decrees in humble calmness, enduring and being humbly confident, taking all things from God and returning them to him, remaining secluded and composed and sinking down into the will of God by abnegating himself and the world? Whoever could achieve this and remain steadfast would in truth consider that God's burden is light; it would, in fact, seem so light, that if all the burdens of the whole world were laid upon his shoulders, they would be as nothing. That blessed man would be glad and overjoyed, feeling as if in heaven, because God would carry the burden and he would be utterly free of it; he would have given up his ground to God, who would step in and direct his doings.

May the supreme God work in us in such a way that his yoke becomes sweet and his burden light. Amen.

SERMON FOR THE SECOND SUNDAY IN LENT

The sermon taken from St Matthew's gospel of the Thursday after the first Sunday in Lent and preached on the second Sunday in Lent, tells the story of the woman of Canaan and how God drives some people by setting the inward man against the outward man. (Matth. 15, 21-29.)

Jesus went from thence and retired into the coast of Tyre and Sidon. And behold a woman of Canaan who came out of those coasts, crying out said to him: Have mercy on me O Lord, thou son of David: my daughter is grievously troubled by a devil. Who answered her not a word. And his disciples came and besought him, saying: Send her away, for she crieth after us. And he answering, said: I was not sent but to the sheep that are lost of the house of Israel. But she came and adored him, saying: Lord, help me. Who answering, said: It is not good to take the bread of the children and to cast it to the dogs. But she said: Yea, Lord, for the whelps also eat of the crumbs that fall from the tables of their masters. Then Jesus answered: O woman, great is thy faith; be it done to thee as thou wilt. And her daughter was cured from that hour.

O children, this gospel shows us the safest way to the most glorious and profitable conversion which can be effected in this temporal world; if, however, we do not, one way or another, take this road, all our efforts will be in vain.

Take the words: 'Jesus went from thence.' From

where did he go out? He left the Pharisees and the scribes. Children, take heed of the reason why he left them. What sort of people were these, whom Jesus left behind? The scribes were the learned men who set great store by their knowledge, whereas the Pharisees were those who thought very highly of their clerical dignity, insisting on their set views and rules. These constitute two of the most blighting motives which can spread in clerical circles; those who persist in fostering them are ruined, because they become corrupted and sink deeper and deeper. Yet there are few people who are not, in one way or another, afflicted with one or both of these evils. The scribes stand for the reasoning people, who judge everything by the rules of reason or the senses; taking in everything by their senses, their reason absorbs it and they make big words, glorying in them, as if they understood great things. But their ground, from which truth should come forth, remains empty and deserted. The others are the Pharisees, the clerics who think highly of their goodness and their dignity, persisting in their rules and views, deeming their customs to be beyond reproach and expecting to be honoured and lauded for their own sakes. Their whole inner ground is filled with contempt for all people who are not as they are. Our Lord Jesus Christ left these people behind him.

They had asked him to give a reason why his disciples did not uphold the good customs of their ancestors but sat down at table with unwashed hands. Our Lord answering, said: 'Why do you not keep God's commandments?' This question is typical of such people's way of thinking: they take their own rules and customs to be of divine origin and of God's will, thereby despising and condemning those noble friends of God who refuse to make their own rules of life because they must follow God on his hidden paths.

By this I do not mean that vain and irresponsible people in a congregation should not be reprimanded; otherwise all moral discipline would go by the board. But beware of the ways of the Pharisees; watch your inner being in case a pseudo-holiness is hiding there, the source and aims of which do not emanate from God. Rest assured that Jesus would not keep company with such hypocrites and would have nothing to do with them. There are some people who lay much stress on the outward appearance of their works and of their mental attitudes: they think that if they appear to be good, all is well. But at the same time their ground is encumbered with worldly ties and choked by weeds; yet of this ground they do not often take stock. The Jews act in the same way; they pray, fast and study, yet their inner ground is not turned towards God, but towards sinful creatures whom they love, desire and listen to, thus wasting many good efforts on them.

No, children, God will not abide with such pharisaical people; those are not the seeds planted by God. Rest assured, they must be pulled out by their roots, as he said: 'He that is not with me is against me; and he that gathereth not with me, scattereth.' When harvest time comes and he gathers his corn, be sure that all those will be abandoned by him who have gathered not with him, but with another master, and all those will be cast out in whose ground he cannot find his plants.

Children, at the present time there are two false principles trying to rule us; they are the merely natural cleverness after the fashion of the scribes, and the hypocritical way of the Pharisees with regard to purely formal doctrines. Nowadays people are so clever after the manner of the scribes that there is hardly one who goes to confession that is not full of tricks and dodges, clinging all the time to his own views. Jesus, in his lifetime, left those people behind, as he assuredly also does now.

Where did he go? He retired into the coast of Tyre and Sidon. Tyre, which means 'distress' and Sidon, which stands for 'being driven'.

Oh, my children, so very few people realise what a splendid thing it is when these two unite. The result is a truly noble one when the soul is hard driven and her reaction is swift.

Then what sort of pursuit is this? It is simply the result of the inner man who wants to be with God where he truly belongs, driving and chasing the outer man in that direction. He, on the other hand is attracted by another path, seeking—because he is mere matter—things of the lower order where he feels most at home. That is why the two sides are always at variance. The essence of the inner man is with God and that is the course which the divine parts of his nature—his wishes, thoughts and his will—tend to follow. This, however, goes against the outer man's inclinations and he fights it, as St Paul says: 'For I know that there dwelleth not in me, that is to say in my flesh, that which is good. For to will, is present with me; but to accomplish that which is good, I find not. For the good which I will, I do not; but the evil which I will not, that

I do.' In this way those two natures chase each other, whilst God and his grace intervene from above, chasing them both. Wherever this driving is fully grasped, things are going well, because 'all who are driven by the spirit of God, are God's children'.

This driving, however, gives rise to great anxiety and distress, but as soon as man is aware of this fear and observes the stirring within himself, he can be certain that Jesus will come and enter into his soul. Jesus will not, however, come to those who do not submit to being driven and who do not feel fear. Such people will never achieve anything, they remain as they are and do not become conscious of themselves; they do not know themselves, nor do they notice temptation when it raises its head, attacking matter and mind. Yet, even those temptations seen in the right light, should make man bow down and adore God, for they are proof that he still directs our life. Unless you heed the danger signal when it lights up, the world with its violent storms, the Fiend with his subtle tricks, the flesh, the senses and particularly the lowest powers will attack you while faintness of heart will make you lean towards material and external things. At the same time, the inner man, by virtue of his inclination towards God, is driven against the outward man's wishes; that this struggle should result in anxiety and distress is only right and just.

What, then, should the poor man do when he is thus caught up in this pursuit and can find no way out? Truly, he should do what the poor woman did: he should go to Jesus and cry with a loud voice— expressing his infinite longing: 'Lord, Son of David, have mercy on me.'

Oh, children, this pursuit gives rise to the surging up of a great sound—as of a raging storm—which, though powerful enough to travel thousands of miles, is gathered into a deep sigh, an abysmal groan, which reaches far beyond nature's bounds and can only reach its culminating point in the Holy Ghost. St Paul said: 'The Holy Ghost prays for us with innumerable sighs.'

Children, this is the best possible way to prepare the ground and no better way can be found in this temporal world. Mark my words: when the poor man, thus driven, sinks in this state of abysmal distress, calling to God with piteous sighs and such great longing that the heavens resound with it, while God pretends that he has either not heard or will have nothing to do with it—man must let this longing return into the ground, there to be endured and formed. Oh children, what could have happened that the Font of perfect Charity should have refused to hear the woman when she called? The Font, the waters of which flowed freely for Adam, was denied to us when he fell. What type of miracle, then, did God hope to find here?

The disciples besought him and spoke against her. At last Jesus said in a harsh voice that he had come to gather the misguided sheep of the house of Israel and 'It is not good to take the bread of the children and cast it to the dogs'. And then, not only did he refuse to help her, but he spoke even more harshly, scolding her and proving to her that it would be an injustice towards the children of Israel if he granted her wish. He not only refused to give her the bread which, as we all know, is a necessary and common thing, but, by calling her a dog, he also denied that she was a child and a human being. How much more could he have tempted and tried her, driving her at the same time nearer to God?

What did she do, when thus pursued? She suffered it and drove herself even deeper down than he had intended to drive her; she sank down into the ground and pressing still farther towards the lowest depths, she said: 'Nay, Lord, not even a dog, only a little whelp.' In spite of being thus engulfed and reduced to nothing, she nevertheless retained her confidence and added: 'Yea, Lord, for the whelps also eat of the crumbs that fall from the table of their masters.'

O, children, who amongst us could probe so deeply into the ground of truth—certainly not with the help of words, definitions or the senses—and sink so deeply into the real ground, that however low God or creatures might want to press him, he would sink even deeper into truth and though they should attempt to deny, crush and expel him, would remain steadfast, pressing down all exterior things deeper than ever and giving his perseverance the chance to rise? If one of us succeeded in this most important of aims, he would indeed have done well. And these are the only paths which in truth lead directly to God. But there are not many amongst us who have this woman's true and real confidence and can thus arrive at such unfathomable self-denial and steadfast adherence to the inner ground.

Therefore she received the answer: 'O woman, great is thy faith, be it done to thee as thou wilt.' And in fact all those who have thus been found just will be given the same answer. All you desire shall be done unto you in the manner you want it done; as you abandon your own self, you come into God's inheritance, but you cannot have what you want as long as you have not severed your earthly ties. Only by denying yourself can you have your wishes granted. In the same measure as man makes way, God in his truth takes charge.

Children, I shall say no more now, only tell you a little story in connection with this matter. I know a woman from Canaan—that is what I shall call her, for this happened four years ago and she is still amongst us—who was in such deep ecstasy and her spirit was carried to such heights that she saw God, our Lady and the saints. But at the same time she caught sight of herself, exceedingly far removed from God, and seeing this, her spirit was gripped by an extraordinarily intense pain, as God's remoteness caused her to be grievously tormented as if she were in hell (the supreme agony of hell consists in the knowledge of having cut oneself off from God). Seized by terror her spirit turned to our Lady and the saints, imploring them to help her. But she saw that their glances were fastened on God and not for one moment did they lend an ear to her supplication; their joy and rapture was so intense that they neither heard nor heeded her cry for help. So, in the manner of human beings she appealed to the suffering of the saints and the agony and wounds of our Lord Jesus Christ; however, she was told that she could not appeal to them, because she had never honoured them. When she saw that neither our Lady and the saints, nor the holy agony of our Lord would come to her aid, she turned to our Lord himself and her human spirit spoke thus: 'Oh, Lord, since nobody will help me I ask you, merciful God, to be mindful that I am your poor creature and you are my God;

pass your sentence according to your most precious will whether or not you want to keep me for ever in this infinite misery of hell. I leave it to you, dear Lord, and your gracious will.' And having thus spoken she let herself sink into the ground of eternity; yet, as soon as she let herself sink down she was immediately lifted across the dividing gap and drawn into the divine abyss, being—as it were—engulfed and absorbed in God's wondrous bounty. O for the blessed joy of this eternal gulf!—This person, who is only a young girl, still experiences day by day the same sinking into the ground and being lifted up again. I honestly believe that never in her life has she committed a grave sin, which would call down on her God's anger. Children, who, then, is to mediate for those who have repeatedly angered God very deeply and who so persistently cling to worldly things?

This human being let herself, for the sake of God, be drawn into an eternity of excruciating pain. But people do not generally do likewise, particularly *not* those who imagine that after four or five years they must arrive at goodness knows what miraculous heights and say: 'Oh, please pray for me that I may become one of the dearest friends of God.' Do not consider yourselves worthy of becoming, of your own will, one of the least. Sit down in the lowest place and according to this gospel, you will be exalted. But those who exalt themselves will be humbled. Desire only what God has decreed in eternity and the place which he has chosen for you in his all-loving will.

In this way, my children, by completely re-nouncing our selves, our ways and possessions we shall truly walk in God. Whosoever could be given one single drop or be touched by one single spark of this renunciation would achieve more and do more good than if he tore the clothes from his body and gave them away or if he ate thorns and stones (even provided that nature could bear it). And to have lived one instant of this life is of more consequence than having lived forty years by one's own rules.

Children, this would be by far the shortest, easiest and most noble of all ways which our mind can perceive.

What are you doing, then, wasting precious time, neglecting the lovely and pure treasure which could and should, without intermission, be born in you, spending the years of your lives running without advancing and being no nearer to perfection than you were when you first started. Surely, that is a deplorable state of things; if only you could see the irreparable harm you are doing!

Let us pray to the Lord that he may immerse us so deeply that we may be found in him. Amen.

SERMON FOR THE SATURDAY BEFORE PASSION SUNDAY

This sermon admonishes us that we should return to our Source and tells us what it is that hinders us in the achievement of this aim. We are also taught how important it is for us to know the difference between a true and a false friend of God. (John 8, 12.)

Our Lord said: 'I am the Light of the world,' but the Jews spoke against him, saying that he was from Galilee and that his own people would have none of him. 'Do not let it trouble you,' he replied, 'I am the Light of the world and of all men.' This Light gives birth to the natural light of the world, such as the sun, the moon and the stars, and it is the Source of the world of the senses as well as being the origin of the spiritual light—the human mind—which guides man when he returns to it; when, however, the mind rejects its origin, it is held captive in a self-inflicted darkness, in sombre contrast to the true Light, the essential Light of the world. Our Lord said that we should renounce our own light which is sheer darkness compared with his Light and is at variance with him, since he is the true Light. He wants to infuse us, so that we may share his splendour with him, with his Being, his life, his bliss and his joy. He also said to his Father: 'That they all may be one, as thou, Father, art in me and I in thee; that they also may be one in us and that they may be made perfect in one.' Though we

38

cannot be one by nature with the Father and the Son,
we can be one with them by the mystery of sanctifying
grace.

We know that the elements such as the earth,
fire and water, return to their origin. How, then,
is it possible that man, this noble creature, the
miracle of miracles, for whose sake God, in his love,
created heaven and earth and all the things therein,
should be so concerned with himself instead of
turning his gaze towards his eternal origin and
Light, and trying to reach his final aim? We must
view this question from two angles. The first one is
the problem of how man can gain re-entry into his
origin and by what ways and means he can achieve
it. The second question is: what is the obstacle which
prevents him from trying to pursue this road and
thereby makes him forfeit the chance of ever reaching
the goal? It must indeed be a great obstacle if it is
able to bar the way to the supreme good and to lead
man astray. There are two kinds of obstacles which
may be observed in two types of people, the first of
which are those whose hearts are obsessed by the
world with its desires and who are content to live
only through the medium of their senses and natural
gifts, thereby destroying their reasoning powers
and frittering away their lives. They remain in
darkness and have a hostile attitude towards the
light. The second type of people are to be found
amongst the clergy, some of whom have famous
names and a striking appearance and think that
they have overcome their natural reluctance to
accepting the light, whereas at heart they are really
self-centred Pharisees, full of self-love and self-will.
When one finds them amongst the Friends of God,

it is very often difficult to detect them, because sometimes they perform more outward exercises than the true friends of God; they pray, watch and fast and lead a life of abstinence so that nobody, except those in whom the Holy Ghost dwells, can recognise them for what they are. There is, however, one unmistakable sign by which the difference between them and the true friends of God can be detected. They always judge other people, but never themselves, and look for the reflection of their own ego in other people—even in God—whereas the true friends of God judge no one but themselves.

Children, this pharisaical way of searching for such self-centred aims has penetrated so deeply into the very nature of these people, that it occupies even the smallest recesses of their being and it would be easier to break down iron barriers than to overcome this obstacle by means of natural resources. There is only one way of removing it: God must take charge and reign supreme in their souls. This, however, is the prerogative of his true friends; the world is so full of these obstacles that we find men and women in all walks of life affected by them, and they do such dreadful damage that the hearts of the true friends of God are pierced with sorrow when they see God being maligned in men's hearts through the evil perpetrated by these Pharisees.

The inner ground of the soul must never be allowed to be inert, for while man lives it can never be completely destroyed or conquered, so long as he keeps on the alert. As it is extremely difficult to accept the true light and to attune oneself to one's origin, many people fall back on their natural resources and remain in that state, because their natural understanding gives them so much satisfaction that all other pleasures which the world can offer are as nothing when compared with it. Nevertheless, even pagans have realised that if they remain in the realm of their natural light and refuse to rise above it, they are doomed to eternal darkness. These, then, are the obstacles which bar the way to the true Light.

There are, however, other means and a shorter way by which one can arrive at the Source and the Light. When man really abnegates himself and offers God a loving and pure inner ground, when he wants to do God's will and not his own, because he only wishes to honour and glorify him, when he seeks direct contact with God and performs those duties which God orders him to do, so that he is in immediate communion with him and is immersed in the inflow and outflow of God's eternal stream of love—then he has chosen the right way. Here also is the cross-road where the true friends of God part company with the false. The false friends regard everything as relating to themselves and accept God's gifts as their due, keeping them for themselves instead of offering them up to God in love and gratitude, renouncing their self-love and becoming absorbed in him. Whosoever can lose himself so wholeheartedly in God is his truest friend; when, however, man shows no inclination to surrender to God, but rather insists on his own self-love and is judged on the merit of that, he will never see the divine, true light. Moreover, one can easily make the fatal mistake of confusing self-love with the true Light, if one does not carefully examine oneself to see whether or not the natural light has taken the place which was intended for God. One can also find out what type of man one is when one is stricken with great suffering; the true friend swiftly turns to God, accepts the suffering as coming from him and therefore shares it with him or even offers it up so completely that his suffering becomes that of God and is eventually turned into joy and happiness. But the false friends react in a pharisaical way when sorrow assails them; they do not know which way to turn, they exhaust themselves searching for comfort and help and when they do not find it, they break down and give way to despair. They will indeed have every reason to grieve when, in the end, they do not find God in their soul, as they have not built their house on the rock—which is Christ— and must therefore fall into the pit.

These people are a thousand times worse off than the everyday people of the world who admit their sinful ways and live in humble fear; as for the common people, they followed our Lord, whereas the Pharisees, the high clergy and scribes who boasted of their holiness, spoke against him and eventually crucified him. One dare not advise them in anything because immediately they either contradict or use abusive language; they behave exactly in the same way as their ancestors did at the time of Christ, when, with his finger, he wrote words into the sand. They would not admit their faults, and when the leader fled the others followed suit, until nobody was left. It is much easier to advise and help simple people, because they acknowledge their faults and therefore fear God and are humble in his sight.

God in his mercy and love sent us great comfort in

the Person of his only-begotten Son, who is to help us to overcome the manifold obstacles. His holy life, his great and perfect virtues, his example, his teaching and his Passion are to free us from ourselves so that we may abandon our dim light for his true Light. He gave us the holy Sacraments; first holy Baptism and Confirmation, then, when we falter on our way, confession and penance, and in addition he gave us his holy Body. Finally he gave us the Sacrament of Extreme Unction. These are powerful guides and greatly help us on the homeward journey to our origin and the Source.

St Augustine used the following metaphor: 'The great Sun begot a minor Sun and overshadowed it with a cloud, not in order to hide it but rather to dim its light, so that we may be able to look upon it.' The great Sun is none other than the heavenly Father, who begot the minor Sun, his Son Jesus Christ. He, although equally divine, humbled himself and became man, not in order to hide from us but rather to make himself as one of us, so that we may be able to see him. He is the true Light, that enlightens every man who comes into this world. The light shineth in the darkness and the darkness did not comprehend it. This light is only given to the poor in spirit who have renounced their self-love and self-will. There are many amongst us who, for forty years and more, have been deprived of this gracious gift and have never come within reach of it; though they know of it, they have acknowledged it only with their sensible faculties and their reason; their inner ground has no notion of it and is not yet able to discern it. My dear children, you must make every effort, spiritually as well as bodily, to let this true light shine upon you in such a way that you are able to discern it and that it leads you towards your Source. Pray and do everything within your power that you may reach this goal. Ask the Friends of God to pray for you and choose your friends amongst people who are close to God, so that they may draw you near to him. May God, who loves us, help us to reach this blessed state. Amen.

SERMON FOR THE TUESDAY BEFORE PALM SUNDAY

This sermon, taken from St John's Gospel and appointed for the Tuesday before Palm Sunday tells us how we should attend every festival with reverence—marriage-feasts or others—how the rules of our holy order are devised with that end in view and how our Lord is secretly with us when we pray. (John 7, 6.)

Our Lord said: 'Go you up to the festival day; my time is not accomplished, but your time is always ready.' What is this feast to which our Lord bids us go, 'because our time is always'? It is the supreme and ultimate feast of eternal life—eternal bliss, as we call it—when God's presence is truly revealed. It is not to be ours here below and the festival we enjoy now is a mere foretaste, a presage, and inward sensing of God's presence in our spirit. Thus, 'our time is always,' when we seek God and have him in mind while we live and work and love and hope, and it should enable us to rise above ourselves and everything that is not of God simply by loving and wanting him 'all the time'. It is an essential part of our human nature that we should all wish to be present at this marriage-feast of eternal life, because it is only natural that everybody should want to go to heaven; but it is not enough just to wish, we must have God in mind and seek him of our own accord. Some people would like to have the fore-taste of the eternal feast; they complain bitterly if it does not

come their way and when their inner ground is not
in a festive mood while they pray, when they cannot
feel God's presence, they lose courage and pray less
and reluctantly, saying that, because they cannot
feel God they dislike their work and their prayers.
We should never behave in this way because even
if we do not feel him, he is still present and
secretly comes to the feast. Wherever God is, there
is a feast and he does not want to stay away or
forego the feast; he must be wherever we seek him
and give him our pure love; even if he is hidden he is
nevertheless present.

The time of which our Lord was speaking when
he said: 'your time to go up is always', is the one
during which we withdraw within ourselves, search
for him in all our deeds and rise above ourselves;
but the decision as to the time when he wants to
reveal himself to us and give us the grace to find
him, must be left to him. Moreover, there is no
doubt that he is present whenever we seek him and
turn our minds towards him; therefore do not give
up your good practices and do not perform them
reluctantly because, even though he may now be
hidden from you, it is certain that you will find him
in the end. The customs, works and exercises of our
holy order all serve this one purpose, as do our
rules, of whatever kind they may be, that we may
love no one but God so that he may prepare his
festival in our inner ground, which must be ready
and bare to receive him. The more the exercises
and rules are obeyed in this spirit, the more praise-
worthy and useful they become, but as soon as they
are done for their own sake they might just as well be
rules of the Old Testament which, with its many

commandments and wearying exercises and despite its great sanctity and good works, cannot itself lead us to salvation, but only prepares the way for the New Testament, which opens the gates and reveals the kingdom of God. The same principle applies to outward practices which only prepare the way and are not the grounds in which the festival can be celebrated. Unless the old law be adapted and absorbed into the new law which, in its turn, must be immersed in the pureness of the soul, it has little or no effect.

Dear children, we have promised to God and affirmed it by solemn vows that we will love and consider him, because we have forsworn and renounced the world in order to be able to serve him unto death. No bishop or priest can release us from this vow which ties us much more firmly than an oath sworn in court. Many people break that oath, but remember, we become guilty of perjury if, consciously and deliberately, we turn our hearts and minds to creatures, when we have promised them to God. This is the reason for the rules of our holy order. Our brethren asked our father, St Dominic, as he lay dying, to explain to them the essential characteristics of the order and the reason for his choice of its rules; although they could see their practical value (we, too, have learned the practical part of the rules) they wanted to understand their intrinsic qualities which had prompted him to choose these particular rules on which to found his order. He explained that he had chosen them because they were fundamentally necessary for the growth of true love for God, for humility, single-mindedness and goodness. These are essential if we

want to love God simply and whole-heartedly and
we need nothing else to achieve this aim. We must
also love our brothers as ourselves, humbly surrender
our mind to God, show merciful understanding for
each other, rid ourselves of all that is not pure and
divine and of all possessions, give up our will, and
be free of all human influences which may lead us
astray, so that God who has implanted his divine
Image into our inner ground, may be made welcome,
reign supreme in it and thereby have his dearest
wish fulfilled.

Dear sisters, this is the only aim of our order, of
all other orders and of all spiritual life; it is at the
root of every monastic discipline, of its rules and
customs. Every hermit and religious lives by it, and
the reason why it has been laid down in rules and
regulations is because the more there are, the better
they will serve to make us love more perfectly and
make use of them more abundantly. This is the
deeper meaning of our rules and if we do not keep
our vows, although they are stricter than those of
other religious orders, we are disloyal to our order;
but when we are faithful to it, we are firmly grounded
in its fundamental aim, as our father St Dominic
intended us to be. Our own and other religious orders
like those founded by St Benedict, St Augustine,
St Bernard and St Francis all have the same fundamental aim in common—the mainspring of every
religious vocation—but each order has its particular
laws and rules.

Dear children, I entreat you to learn thoroughly
the fundamental rules which teach you that you
must love God and all things which help you on the
way towards that love, so that God can really and

truly celebrate his festival with you. You must also obey your own rules by attending choir, singing and studying, whether or not it comes easily or causes you trouble; be in a festive frame of mind, rather than in a heavy and unwilling one, so that you neither miss nor are deprived of the marriage-feast of eternal life. Although it is quite true that, when man is free of mortal sin and is firmly resolved to do nothing against God's will, he will be safe in our holy faith, but you can rest assured that, if he wants to go to this festival of love where God's presence is felt and discerned, he must offer God a free and pure inner ground; then God will reveal himself to man, imbuing him with his Spirit. You can only speak of a true devotion when you enjoy nothing and have no longing for anything except loving and contemplating God. That was the call of God's love when he gave us our vocation and we must obey our calling, because God delivered us from a wicked and deceitful world and led us to the pure life of penance although by nature we are the children of wrath and perdition and our ways make us only worthy of eternal damnation.

St Augustine said: 'Man is made of foul, evil-smelling and corrupt matter, a clod made of clay whose end is eternal death. This fate can be overcome by a life of penance to which God has called and invited you, out of his free and pure love, without merit on your part.' But what is really the essence of such a penitential life? It is no more and no less than a complete renunciation of everything which is not of God and an absolute concentration on the true perfection which is God. The further you go on this road, the more penance you will do.

It is only right and just that, filled with awe at the thought of God's mercy, you should thank him that he invited and called you to his service, because now you have every reason to hope that he wants to keep you by his side for all eternity, all the more so as he has brought you here, away from the wicked world, and has chosen you as his brides, offering to receive you into his intimate circle of friends. It is quite evident that it is God in his true presence who chooses us and he also manifests himself when he compels young people, who by nature are unruly and inclined to love the world, to curb their passions and be so captivated by God that they follow him, leaving all natural ties behind; were it not for God, who is secretly present in their souls, it would be impossible for them to subject themselves to him so completely, because at first they have little knowledge of him.

Well, now it all rests with you! Do your utmost and devote your whole strength to the effort, so that this marriage-feast may be effected, that you may discover God in your soul and that he may find you in a happy and joyful disposition. He will celebrate the feast in you, if you, with a firm will, withdraw within yourselves during your prayers and work which, after all, are only part of your duties; it is when a human being feels that he belongs to God and to no one else, that God's loving presence is made manifest in the feast which unites man to God. Truly, we are of God and when he has united himself with us he does not deprive us of his presence, but rather by that fusion endows us with his attributes. Is it not a wonderful thing, a joyful and blessed life when we are in God and God is in us, in time and in eternity?

May God in his mercy help us to reach this aim. Amen.

SERMON FOR THE FRIDAY BEFORE
PALM SUNDAY

This is the sermon taken from the Gospel of St John about the words which Caiphas spoke: 'It is expedient that one man should die for the people.' The sermon deals with three different ways in which men should mortify their own will in order to enter into eternal life. (John 11, 47.)

St John, in his gospel, tells us that Caiphas said: 'You know nothing, neither do you consider that it is expedient for you that one man should die for the people and that the whole nation perish not.' He did not say this of his own will, but the Holy Ghost spoke through him and it was the last prophecy spoken before the death of our Lord. Caiphas also said: 'This man doth many miracles. If we let him alone, all will believe in him and the Romans will come and take away our place and nation.'

Let us ponder on the inconceivably deep love of which Jesus Christ gave proof when he crowned the supreme act of love by dying for us, when his spiritual and physical strength, his inner and outer senses were subjected to the most terrible suffering.

There are many people who would like to know of a short cut to arriving at the most intimate revelations. Let us consider whether this can be done. Our Lord calls to himself three types of people. He calls the man who is an obvious sinner in order to save his inner ground and to prepare it anew. When the humble man sees this happening, he thanks Providence and rejoices greatly; but there are those who would rather run down that person and let their senses pass judgement on him. They do so to their own detriment.

The second type of person God draws to himself with the help of penance. What exactly is penance? When, for instance, you would like to speak but keep silent instead, or when you would like to cast longing glances, but rather close your eyes and refrain from looking—in short, you do penance when you keep away from the things which give your senses the greatest pleasure, when you turn away from them and shut yourselves off.

The third type is drawn to God directly, through his own self. As you know, man must continually die unto himself. What is it in man that must die? It is self-will and self-reliance. Nothing you have achieved by your own will, even if it were the martyrdom of all the martyrs, or the accumulated charity of all Christians of all ages: nothing for which you have a liking or which satisfies you will be of any use to you. What, then, must we acquire so that man in us may die? Were you to die a thousand deaths a day and be re-awakened again, were you to ask to be drawn and quartered time and again, were you to eat thorns and stones—all these efforts could not obtain it for you. No, you must sink into God's deep ineffable mercy, calmly humbling your will before God and creatures and make sure that Jesus Christ grants it to you by the sheer power of his meekness, absolving goodness, mercy and love. He expressed it quite clearly when he said: 'When you shall have done all things that are commanded you, say: We are unprofitable servants, we have done that which we ought to do.'

But should man not die unto himself, 'the Romans will come and occupy the city.' What else does Rome symbolise than the highest worldly ambitions? Vainglory—vice of all vices—occupies the city, which ought to be Christ's, and kills the people—in other words the forces, high and low, the soldiers and servers of the soul.

O children, take good care! There are many strange people in this world who try to bypass this noble path by affecting a grand manner and giving themselves great airs. Be sure that as long as the man in us does not die, he spreads across all the forces of the inner and the outer man, destroying the very soil in which Jesus Christ ought to plant his seed. We know of so many men who seemed so great and in whom God had begun such auspicious work, but who were ruined in just this way. Take Solomon, for instance, to whom God spoke, his son, and Samson who received the angel's message. How deep was their fall! Because the man did not die in them they used God's gifts to enhance their conceit and were ungrateful to him. How terrible was God's judgement in the end! So dreadful was it that the Church is doubtful whether they are saved.

The 'very clever' people must also be dealt with. They have developed only by their natural reason and they pretend to have reached beyond all things. Children, you must take no notice of them. What nature gives she reclaims and what Christ gives, returns unto himself. These highly intellectual people, influenced by their senses, are far more prone to take offence than noble and calm people. These often hear the latter's reproach: 'Gracious me, what an irritable person you are!' when in reality they remain in tranquillity in their inner ground. Actually, the hardship of this deceptive impression to which God subjects the inner man, fills him with great contentment because he realises that God has much more confidence in his endurance than in that of the outward man. Children, be not bewildered and keep near to God. You have your ideal in Jesus Christ who sweated blood and water when his human nature was in agony. Dearest children, you must also learn to suffer in the same way, lying prostrate under God and creatures, but, above all, do not draw away from God, for every death is followed by eternal life.

The Father, the Son and the Holy Ghost help you and me that we may die in this manner. Amen.

SERMON FOR THE SUNDAY OF THE ASCENSION OF OUR LORD

This is an interpretation of the Ascension of our Lord and of five types of captivity in which people in this temporal world are held; it also speaks of the means by which the Evil Spirit captures them and in what way they can free themselves. (Eph. 4, 8.)

Our Lord Jesus Christ ascended into heaven and took captivity with him, itself held captive. We find five different types of captivity to which people in this world are subjected and which Christ removes and takes with him, when he rises within us.

The first type is that of man when, through love, he is chained to creatures, be they alive or dead; in neither case does his love belong to God. Just because this love for human beings comes so naturally —they are attracted to each other by the similarity of their nature—the damage done is inconceivable. It affects people in two different ways. In the first case they are sufficiently self-conscious to see the danger; they are distressed, their conscience pricks them and thus they are punished. This is a good sign because it shows that God has not abandoned them; he makes them suffer incessantly, day and night, even while they eat and drink. If they do not close their ears but heed the call, they will yet go to heaven. Others, however, move about quite freely in this harmful captivity, they are completely deaf and blind, well content and even eager to do the right thing. They perform many good works, they can sing or be silent, they can read holy books and help others and even say many prayers, so that they may improve through their deeds and be permitted to rejoice in God and the world; thus they are always rather devout, mournful at times, yet usually very happy. But such people as these are in rather a precarious position, because the Enemy so treats them, that he may hold them in captivity; nature also deceives them, and in this way they are greatly and dangerously tempted.

They would reap more benefit if they were sorely afflicted and overcome by grief and woe, because they would then rid themselves of this dangerous and detrimental captivity. But if they persist in it until they die, they are sure to remain the Devil's captives for all eternity and no power will be able to come to their rescue.

The second type of captivity is inflicted on some people who, as soon as they are delivered from the first captivity—outward love for creatures—fall into the vice of self-love. This love fills them with so much righteousness that it makes you wonder. Nobody, not even themselves, rebukes them, they put up such a wonderful show and have such splendid delusions that nothing can touch them. In the course of time their self-love seeks in all their actions their own profit, pleasure, consolation, comfort and honour, and so deep do they sink into themselves, that they search for that and for nothing else whenever they look about them, even when they look for God. Oh, what would come to light, if one could reach their ground! What appears to be great sanctity, will perforce turn out to be a treacherous ground. Oh, how difficult it will be to help these people when they approach the true spirit with their spoilt nature and reasoning arguments—how hard will it be to deliver them from their captivity!

When someone is thus captivated by nature, who can help him? Surely no one but God himself. So many things seem to them a necessity, their needs are so manifold and they fancy that they are so weak, so delicate. But when it happens, as it sometimes does, that their worldly attachments—be they comfort, friends, goods or some other precious thing—are called in question or taken away from them, more often than not they are angry and abandon God, their actions are no longer good or they speak untrue or ignorant things about him. And then man is no longer human, but only a mad dog or a ravenous wolf. This self-love is a very injurious captivity.

The third kind of captivity is that of the reason. This is the downfall of many people, because they destroy everything—be it a doctrine or some truth— which should be born in the spirit, by dragging it down to the level of their reasoning powers, so that whatever it is, they may understand it rationally and be able to expound it, thereby giving themselves airs and adding to their self-importance; in this way they never achieve anything, they neither perform good deeds, nor do they have life. They also view our Lord Jesus Christ's loving Image through the eyes of reason; were they to transfer their conception of it into the divine supernatural light, they would soon see the difference; it would seem like the light of a candle as compared to the sunlight, although the difference between natural and supernatural light is still considerably greater. The natural light—in contrast to the divine light—only shines outwardly; it is reflected in pride, conceit, in the praise of others and in the judging of our fellow-men. Also it only concentrates on the exterior of things, thereby satisfying the senses and sentiments. On the other hand, the divine light, which is born of truth and presses itself down into the ground, believes and knows itself to be the least, the meanest, weakest and blindest amongst all; that is right and proper, for whatever its nature, it belongs to God. Also it tends towards the interior, not the exterior, searching for and using its entire strength in order to reach for the inward ground from whence it came. All activities of these men are performed with their minds turned towards their roots to which they do their utmost to return as soon as possible. That is also why there is a great difference between those who try to live according to holy Scripture and those who merely read in it. Those who read it wish to be exalted and honoured and look upon those who live it as absurd and foolish beings whom they condemn, persecute and curse. The people, however, who live by it, regard themselves as sinners and have pity on the others. And the two different ways to which they come in the end stand in even greater contrast to each other than their ways of life did. Whereas the one type finds Life, the other finds eternal death. St Paul said: 'For the letter killeth, but the spirit quickeneth.'

The fourth captivity is that of sweet raptures of the spirit. Many a man, attuned to God, loses his way in this captivity because he pursues the sweetness too long and surrenders to it in an undisciplined manner, searching for and holding on to it too eagerly, because it seems a good thing and delightful to possess. But that is the moment when nature claims her share and man is deprived of the delight, just when he thinks that he has grasped God. It is an easy matter to make the test and recognise whether it was God's or nature's delight; just watch the man and see whether he is restless, discontented and troubled as soon as the sweetness is taken away from him and whether he is unable to serve God as willingly and loyally as when he still possessed it. If the sweetness was not sent by God the man could still come to grief even if he had enjoyed it for forty years or more and then lost it. Moreover if he has reached the highest grade of the sweetness and persevered, it still depends on God's decision whether or not he will save the man: he might yet be lost.

The fifth captivity is that of man's own will inasmuch as he also wants to have his own will in divine matters, even with God himself. But then, if God were to dwell in this man's very will and desires, so much so that he became rid of all his faults and gained all virtue and perfection—surely it would seem foolish if he were to reject this his will. Yet I have thought better since. Even if I could have my will and desires with God as I have described them I would still say: No, Lord, not according to my grace (or gifts, or will), but I shall accept and carry out your will, Lord, as if it were mine; should it be your will that I have nothing, I shall accept it and go hungry. By accepting poverty in real tranquillity one has more profit and receives more, than if one takes according to one's own will.

It is far more beneficial to man if, instead of using his own will, whether it be to grasp God or creatures, he renounces it in meekness and humility, forsaking his own will and accepting all things in true calmness. That is why I prefer a really tranquil man who is less active and has less pretences, to a man who seems much greater if judged by his actions, his appearance and his big notions, but who is much less tranquil.

While our Lord was still with his disciples they were filled with such wondrous love for his humanity that they could not attain to his divinity. Then he said: 'It is expedient to you that I go; for if I go not the Paraclete will not come to you.' After this they had to wait for forty days until he was lifted up to heaven, when he took with him and glorified all that was best in them; yet it was only after another ten days that the Holy Ghost, the true Comforter was sent to them. What were days for them, are years for us. Their period of waiting was shortened, one day counted as much as a year because they were God's elect and chosen to form the foundation of the Church. Man may do whatever he likes, he may try as hard as he can, but he will find it very difficult to arrive at true peace or be really godly until he reaches his fortieth year. Up to then he is troubled by many things, nature drives him hither and thither and is his master while he imagines that he is obeying God's commands; thus he cannot arrive at true and perfect peace nor be in harmony with God. After that time he shall wait another ten years ere he is filled with the Holy Ghost, the Comforter, the Spirit who teaches all things. The disciples had to wait another ten days in spite of their having been prepared through their way of life, their sufferings and their renunciation of all things they had left behind and although they were supremely qualified inasmuch as they had parted with the One whom they had loved above all, for whose sake they had left everything and who had taken with him into heaven their minds, hearts, souls and love, all of which were blessed in him and with him. After all the anticipation and the noble lessons they had been taught, they still had to wait ten more days before they received the Holy Ghost. So they waited, recollected and closed in. Man must do likewise. When, at the age of forty he has reached a certain composure, attained a state of godliness and more or less overcome nature, he needs ten more years—until he has reached his fiftieth year—before the Holy Ghost's highest and most noble wisdom can be his. During these ten years in which man is becoming godly and is overcoming nature, the Holy Spirit teaches him the ways of truth. That is the moment when man should endeavour to re-collect himself, to sink down and be infused into the pure, divine, simple and innermost Truth, where life's noble spark is immersed in its original Power. If the return to that Source is truly accomplished all sins are wiped out even if their number had been legion, and then all grace and bliss flows into man's soul. Then he really is a godly man, a pillar supporting the world and the Church. Amen.

SERMON FOR WHIT-SUNDAY

This interpretation of the meaning of Pentecost, taken from the Gospel of St John, 10, 1-10, tells how the sheep must enter the sheepfold by the door—which is Christ—how we must have God's pure mind, not ours, at heart and must not pay attention to the comforts of life. We should also refrain from judging other people's ways of life.

Our Lord Jesus spoke thus to his beloved disciples: 'He that entereth not by the door into the sheepfold, but climbeth up another way, the same is a thief and a robber. But he that entereth in by the door is the shepherd of the sheep. To him the porter openeth; and the sheep hear his voice and he calleth his own sheep by name and leadeth them out. And when he hath let out his own sheep he goeth before them and the sheep follow him, because they know his voice. But a stranger they follow not but fly from him, because they know not the voice of strangers.' This proverb Jesus spoke to them. But they understood not what he spoke to them. Jesus therefore said to them again: 'I say to you, I am the door of the sheep. All others, as many as have come are thieves and robbers and the sheep heard them not. I am the door. By me, if any man enter in, he shall be saved; and he shall go in and go out and shall find pastures. The thief cometh not but for to steal and to kill and to destroy. I am come that they may have life and may have it more abundantly.' These are the words of our dear Lord according to St John.

Our Lord said that he was the door of the sheepfold. What is this sheepfold, this dwelling of which our Lord is the door? It is the Father's heart, into which Christ's love truly leads us, the door which his loving heart has reopened for us, after it had been locked for so long. In this dwelling all sheep—the saints—are assembled. The shepherd is the eternal Word, the door is Christ's humanity and we assume that the sheep are the human souls, although the angels, too, are part of the fold. The eternal Word has paved the way for all rational creatures, so that they may enter this lovely dwelling of which the Word is the just and good shepherd. And the Holy Ghost is the *hostiarius*, the janitor of the dwelling, as both St Ambrose and St Jerome assert when they say that it is the Holy Ghost who inspires men when they understand and preach the truth. During these days of Pentecost we have spoken of the way in which the Holy Ghost never tires of pulling, coaxing, driving and chasing the heart of men; those amongst you who have studied themselves know it only too well. How tenderly and lovingly he opens the door to the Father's heart, disclosing all the hidden treasures, the secrets and riches of the dwelling. The way in which God's purity, eagerness, yearning and responsiveness reach out to meet man is well beyond all human understanding. And yet, children, how rudely do we refuse this gracious invitation, turning our backs on his urging and yearning, time and again flagrantly denying him admittance. It is recorded in the book of Esther how King Asuerus sent word to his queen requesting her to come and eat with him. But when she refused to appear at his feast, he rejected her and cast her away, banning her from his sight for ever. He chose another woman, who was called Esther, to take her place. Oh, dear children, how many of the Holy Ghost's admonitions and invitations are thus disregarded and brushed aside by human beings who resist and keep him at a safe distance; is it not sad that whenever God wants us, we want something else?

The janitor calls on his own sheep and so does the shepherd—the eternal Word of the Father—who calls them by name and shows them the way. He goes first and they follow after him. When the shepherd calls and leads his own sheep, where does he take them? To his dwelling place. When he goes ahead so that they may follow him, where do they go? Into the fold, the Father's heart where the shepherd's true Being dwells in his eternal home. And all who want to come after him, must enter through the door, which is Christ's humanity. Those amongst the sheep who are his own neither seek nor consider their own profit, all their thoughts and quests are for ever turned to God and his will. He shows them the way and they follow after him; they would not follow a stranger, but would rather flee from him, yet they follow the shepherd, whose voice they know.

If, as Christ said, he is the true door and all those who enter by another way are murderers and thieves —who, then, are those thieves? They are the type of people who insist on relying entirely on their natural quickness of wit which they use to enter the fold. Their mind is not purely and simply attuned to God, nor do they follow the loving example of our Lord Jesus Christ; they are not calm and humble and full of contempt for themselves, nor do they despise their wretched and sinful nature and therefore they are the people who climb up by another way into the fold. But what precisely is it that makes such a thief of man? Deeply concealed in human nature lies a serpent, feigning to be captivated by humility, yet in reality lying in wait, ready to seize upon such spiritual notions as can be grasped by reason and presenting them in an earthly disguise, so that man, whenever he succeeds in something, has the impression that it was achieved by his own wit. This is the way in which they want to acquire pleasures, comfort, tastes and feelings; they wish to be great, holy and blessed, to see and to know and always be in the limelight, yet they are never prepared to abandon themselves. They are the thieves who, with fiendish means, steal in, deprive God of his glory and rob mankind of truth and perfection. Dear children, these thieves do more harm to men than all the thieves who have ever been hanged could have done. Look out for them, take heed and be on your guard against them.

And what of the 'murderer' of whom Christ spoke? It is the untold damage done when we judge other people; though it lies dormant in every one of us, some people are full of it. It is part of the human make-up that people always want to correct others, but cannot see their own faults, because they are so absorbed in the task of judging the others. One man is supposed to talk too much, another one too little, one eats too much, the next one too little, one complains too much, the other one too little. This deadly judgement is applied to all things and is often followed by a scornful attitude towards the other man's heart and inner self. But when it is expressed in bad temper and angry words, it inflicts a fatal wound on the victim, just as it previously wounded the aggressor, when he was someone else's victim. Now the other man is induced likewise to take his turn in passing judgement on somebody else and kills him as well, because he, too, will be susceptible to attacks by word or tempers. What exactly do you know of your neighbour's inner ground? How can you tell God's will with regard to him or in which particular way God has called or invited him? Do you dare to take upon yourself to judge his works, do you try to direct and rule him after your own ideas, thereby murdering God's will and inflicting your false verdict on your neighbour? This murderer causes untold harm amongst God-seeking people and does not give heed to God's words: 'Judge not that you may not be judged. For with what judgement you judge, you shall be judged, and with what measure you mete, it shall be measured to you again.' We ought not to condemn anything, except mortal sin. But should we, through circumstances, be forced to sit in judgement, we should appeal to the Holy Ghost to use us as his mouth-piece. We should choose a proper time and place, do the judging humbly and gently, not inflicting ten new wounds by trying to heal one old one and not storm at the culprit in a violent rage, but show him lovingly and with patience where he went wrong. Whosoever does not do it in this spirit, remains in the shadow and has no part in the true light. Dear children, know and judge yourselves and remember that during the whole course of your lives you are burdened with a sinful nature and therefore, if you want to reach this blessed fold, be your own judges

and leave your neighbour to make his peace with
God, and God with him. Remember, too, that in the
same measure as you have disdained people and
raised yourselves above them by finding fault with
them, you will be made subject to others and the
same treatment will be meted out to you.

When, however, man takes this murderer in hand,
turning in upon himself in order to judge himself
in an ardent, deep and inner realisation of his own
being, the murderer finds the thief hiding in the
ground; this thief, under the disguise of righteousness, stole and continues to rob man's true spirit of
God's grace and the great treasures hidden in his
plenitude, by unlawfully appropriating and abusing
these divine gifts. But when the thief is brought
before the murderer and rebuked for the damage he
has done, when he is captured and it so happens,
as it sometimes does, that these two fight and stab
each other so that both are killed, then, children,
when both the thief and the murderer are dead and
all judging has died with them, what a wonderful
result that will yield! Then all verdicts will return
to God, into his justice, his will and into his essence,
to be administered how, where and when he chooses.

Children, if both the thief and the murderer
were dead, true and real peace would reign in that
man's breast; he would be blessed, would enter the
fold by the true door, the janitor would open it for
him and he would be admitted into the Father's
infinite grounds, where he could go in and go out
and always find ample pastures. Infinitely solaced,
he would sink into the Godhead and come forth
again, full of love and joy, to delight in the holy,
deified and all-loving humanity. God's words, which

he spoke through the mouth of the prophet Joel[1] would indeed come true. 'I will feed my sheep and let them rest, when work and rest will be one and the same and I shall lead them upon the mountains of Israel to the green grass of the fat pastures. I will feed my own.'

This loving and noble shepherd, the eternal Word, leads his beloved sheep, they follow him, but would follow no stranger; they are given the most precious food in full measure, so that they may profit by it and be blessed in God's eternal glory.

May God grant us that we shall advance thus far. Amen.

[1] The Quotation is actually taken from Osee.

SERMON FOR TRINITY SUNDAY

This interpretation of Holy Trinity shows that every human being must centre on two faculties, one of which testifies for and the other against him, if he is to achieve noble ends; to achieve this, he must die many deaths, accept grief with joy and bitterness with a sweet temper. (Luke 18, 9.)

This is the wonderful day when we celebrate the joyful and greatly revered feast of the Holy Trinity. All the feasts, high and low, which we have so far celebrated this year compare with the present one as the flower with the fruit; they all contributed towards to-day's feast which is the aim and reward of the labour. I can think of no adequate words with which to speak of it, because it is far beyond words and expression, transcending ineffably all angelic and human understanding. The difference between the understanding of a seraphim of the highest order and that of an ass is negligible when one compares it with the manner in which this feast transcends all understanding. That is why St Dionysius wrote: 'Whatever one may say of it comes nowhere near the truth, but is as near to a lie as to the truth.'

Some ignorant people, however, act as if they had understood every morsel of it and speak in well-turned phrases about something which cannot be expressed in human language. No, dear children, don't concern yourselves with too deep a wisdom, as St Paul said, but leave the high clerics to study and discuss it, because, in spite of their lack of divine understanding, the Church must permit them to speak for her, so that she should not fall prey to heresies; you, however, are not allowed to do it.

Christ said: 'We speak what we know and we testify what we have seen.' Children, apart from Christ in his divinity, none of us 'knows' or 'has seen' and therefore we can only arrive at understanding by way of Jesus Christ testifying for us. He does so in two ways, helping and halting—with his highest and his lowest forces—but if one of us should be without one of the powers of testifying, he will not achieve his objective as the two faculties are just like two forces running parallel in man, who is not to follow one and then the other but must let them act concurrently within him. Man should be found to be the same in peace and in adversity, he should be at peace in strife, accept grief with joy and bitterness with sweet patience. But, children, this virtue can neither be found in the outward man nor in nature, but can only be achieved by sanctifying grace. Many a bitter death—adversities—must ravage nature (for we owe God more than one death) each of which is followed by a glorious and divine life, if only we are conscious of it.

Children, such life and death as well as such perfections as we lack can be achieved by frequent and efficient mental prayer, when it is offered up with great sincerity. The serene mind loves and considers both the even and the uneven in every human being; many people would like to follow God as long as the path is smooth, but as soon as the going becomes rough they turn back. The rough path, however, is by far the more fruitful, profitable and the better one, because it leads to the intrinsic Truth. The easy way—as it were—is the flower whereas the difficult one is the fruit. The easy one serves to pave the way, helping and strengthening man to face the trials of the difficult path which, when it is surmounted, leads to his re-birth. This smooth way, however much it serves fruition, does not itself bear fruit. Nobody is ready to love and contemplate God while things go smoothly; if anything, one is inclined to disregard him, although by acting thus one is not testifying for Jesus Christ. We must become truly poor in spirit, infinitely calm yet burning with love; we should suffer inward and outward trials and tribulations and be subjected by men, the flesh and the Enemy to temptations both in body and mind. But should we have succeeded in overcoming these temptations and leaving them behind us, even so we ought to ask them to return in order that, as it were, they may scrape off and carry away the rust they brought with them and which accumulated in the days of sin. It is very likely that a good, pure and spiritual person is more conscious of his sins, and that both his mind and his body react more vividly and definitely to them than do those of a great and persistent sinner; the good man experiences the bitterness of sin and thus attains to perfection. He is admitted into eternal life whereas the wicked and unjust man who does not face his temptations goes to his eternal death.

Why is there such a vast difference between those two men who, though both disfigured by sin, have such a different approach to it? The good man suffers it for the sake of God and his inner ground and his intentions are pure; he accepts the rough with the smooth and gives himself up to God. But the wicked man does not think of God and falls a prey to the temptations peculiar to his personality. Whatever he may receive from God, he wishes it were something else. He would be well satisfied if he could own many things without having to work hard and pay for them. O children, there is nothing you could not achieve if you loved God with a pure heart and kept him always in mind. Then nothing could harm you; all the devils from hell with their spite and the whole world with its filth could pass through your bodies, your soul, your blood and your bones. As long as it happened against your will, it could do you no harm, in fact it would do you much good, if, purely and solely, you had God in mind, not considering yourselves in any way, but only taking the good with the bad and doing his will.

This is what Christ meant when he said: 'Unless a man be born again of water and the Holy Ghost, he cannot enter into the kingdom of God.' We assume that the spirit stands for the evenness and the water for the unevenness. Apart from the soul-destroying dissimilitude of this world, there is an inner, pure and noble unevenness—sorrow as it were—which was born of the outer one. Whosoever could truly endure it, would disclose and reveal a comprehension of the unutterable sorrow—to which created beings can never attain—because the mind, purified by the vagaries of our nature, loves and prefers the inner unevenness, feeling more satisfaction and being more sensitive to it than to all the evenness it could grasp and hold. The clearer, more naked and open this suffering reveals itself, the more intimate will be the fusion with joy. It was because

Lucifer refused to accept humbly the suffering, and was set on having joy only, that he lost the balance between rough and smooth and with it for evermore the chance of feeling joy, whereas the angels acknowledged their suffering and thus sank down into the unutterable joy.

What wonderful fruit the ground of the soul could yield if the serene mind would love and sink into suffering, merging into the true cognisance of its own sorrow and evaluate the treasure it has laid up in the divine abyss! After man has disciplined and purified his nature and his mind as best he can, this sinking down becomes one act of love; when nature has done all within its power and can do no more, it reaches its highest peak and approaches the divine abyss, the sparks of which kindle the spirit so that, helped by the power of supernatural inspiration, it is drawn out of its orbit into the one, pure and unutterable awareness of God. Then the mind soars far above the material world, because it is infused with divine strength and this inner retreat is beyond all human understanding, wonderful and incomprehensible. Although this withdrawal stands out amongst all other experiences, nevertheless each good intention, opinion and wish, each good word and deed, every suffering and distress, have contributed towards it. It could not have been effected by angels, saints, heaven or earth, only by the immeasurable divine abyss; it is far above all nature, the divine ground stretching into the limitless regions beyond all human measure. Thus the serene and pure mind sinks into the divine darkness, into utter silence and an incomprehensible union, where it loses all sensation of joy or suffering, where the mind loses itself, knowing neither God, itself, joy or sorrow or anything else, just sinking into unison with God and losing all power of discernment.

Dear children, if man wants to go thus far he must die unto himself and the world and live a pure life entirely dedicated to God. He must not live for his senses, pursuing this, that, or the other aim, nor be interested in a variety of outward things; although they may seem to be good works, they still greatly hinder those who live purely in and for God, who see him in all things and all things in him. Thus one may arrive at this wonderful and glorious Holy Trinity on which I am too weak and wretched to expound.

May God help us so that all this should also happen to us. Amen.

SERMON FOR THE FEAST OF CORPUS CHRISTI

This is an interpretation of the Feast of the Blessed Sacrament which shows us three degrees of divine praises yielding very good results. It also shows how every man, according to his way of life and disposition, should be willing to receive frequently the holy Food. (John, 6, 56.)

This is the great day when we celebrate the noble feast of the Sacrament of the holy Body of Christ. Although we assemble every day of the year— especially on Maundy Thursday—to celebrate it, our holy Mother the Church has nevertheless ordered that on this day we should be stirred anew and exhorted again to offer veneration and heartfelt gratitude to his holy Body and, as is the custom on great feasts, honour God by renewing our adoration. By fixing this feast, the Church has proclaimed her intentions, and now the people manifest their veneration of the Blessed Sacrament in many ways and by a number of outward activities. It is carried in procession from church to church, the monstrance is adorned with silver and gold, the church bells ring, the people sing, the organs peal and all the people join in the great rejoicing.

Dear children, all this adds to the praise which our soul should offer to God and nothing is too small to contribute towards this aim. But all these outward expressions are of an inferior kind of praise, which we can give to God since our adoration must be expressed in whichever way is possible. There is no little worm so small that, were it endowed with reason, it would not be justified in lifting its head and bowing it in his honour; no created thing is too small to do him homage.

There is another, higher degree of divine praise which consists in man's using his whole reason and judgement in order to proclaim God's glory, letting the expression of his great love well up from the bottom of his heart. This is far more than anything which outer deeds can achieve.

There is yet a third and higher degree of praise. When man once acknowledges that God is so great and he himself so small that he cannot even praise God, this veneration eclipses all words, thoughts and understanding. There was one master who said: 'Man conveys the loveliest things about God when, overwhelmed by the knowledge of his innermost riches, he keeps silent about God.' There was a master who praised God in words, but another master who heard him, rebuked him, saying: 'Be quiet, you are blaspheming,' and they were both right. It is an amazing fact that the ineffable Goodness, which surpasses all angelic and human understanding should be so great that there is no hope of ever expressing it in words. This kind of homage stands infinitely higher than the first two. The soul's cognisance of God's greatness and inexpressible glory is so pure that it is devoid of all expression; it sinks and melts so completely into him that if words could be found to express its praise and gratitude, they would be God's own words. If man could ever be so totally absorbed it would be inconceivable that God could ever abandon him.

Our dear Lord said: 'My flesh is meat and my Blood is drink indeed. He that eateth my flesh and drinketh my Blood abideth in me and I in him.' Do you notice the deep humility of our Lord? He does not mention the sublime element of his Person but only speaks of the substance least valued. This sublime element is his hallowed divinity and though he only speaks of his Body and Blood, his divinity and holy Soul are as real as flesh and blood. His ineffable and supranatural love is seen in its true light when we realise that not only did he become our brother, taking unto himself our sick and corrupt nature— because he became man so that man should become God—but not being satisfied with that, he also resolved to become our Food. That is why St Augustine said: 'There is no family as great as the Christian family, because no other one is as near to their God, as God is to the Christians.' We consume our God as food. What a wonderful love he must have had to have found this means of communion! His love surpasses all human senses and stands so exceedingly high above our love that it ought to pierce all human hearts.

There is no material thing to which man stands in such an intimate and near relation as food and drink, which enters the body through the mouth; in order to unite himself with us in the way nearest to our human nature he thought of this wonderful plan.

But now we must speak about the bodily food and although it may sound coarse it will nevertheless make the following point clearer. St Bernard said: 'When we eat this food we are being eaten.' The food we eat first enters through the mouth, is chewed and then slips gently through the throat into the stomach where it is consumed by the heat of the liver. The stomach boils the food, as it were, separating the coarse—the evil—from the good parts. If man eats as much as one pound of food, only a tiny fraction of it is retained by his nature, all the rest is digested by the stomach and disposed of in different ways. When it reaches the stomach it still consists of three parts which are then boiled and digested by the natural heat; afterwards a high spiritual force, appointed by God for this purpose, divides it amongst the head, the heart and the limbs whence it becomes flesh and the blood which passes through the veins. It is the same with the Body of our Lord. As the bodily food is changed within us, so man who consumes the holy Food, is changed into it. Our Lord spoke thus to St Augustine: 'It is not I who will be changed into you, but you will be changed into me.' This Food passes through the veins into man's inner ground whenever he receives it in a devout manner.

Let us now consider St Bernard's words: 'The food we eat is first chewed and then sinks gently into the body.' What, then, is this chewing? St Bernard says: 'When we consume God, we are consumed by him.' When does God consume us? It is done when he punishes us for our shortcomings, when he opens our inner eyes and shows us where we have failed; in the same way as the food is churned in the mouth by the chewing motion, he chastises our conscience, driving us from great fear and anguish into sorrow and affliction, so that we do not know what will become of us.

My dear children, suffer all these trials, let God consume you, do not hinder him by forcing his action and thereby hastening it, so that you should soon be delivered of the chastisement and able to confess yourselves. You might then be under the false impression that God has accomplished his work in you whereas in reality you wish to resist the chastisement. No! Begin by confessing your sins to God and do not keep on repeating your set prayers, but rather say with a deep sigh coming from the bottom of your heart: 'Oh God, be merciful to me a sinner.' Remain secluded and rest assured that you are faring a thousand times better than if you read learned books and did goodness knows what in order to avoid the chastisement. But be careful that the Enemy does not attack you, diverting your sorrow from its ordered course. He loves to intersperse it with his evil and bitter herbs. But our Lord's herbs are sweet and good and after his chastisement we are filled with a delicious tranquillity, a lovely confidence, trust and hope. Thus we are swallowed up by God. When your food is well chewed it slides with ease and sinks down into the stomach; when your conscience is thoroughly chastised and purified and you continue in your utter confidence, trusting implicitly in our Lord, you too are gently swallowed up. This is the examination of conscience of which St Paul speaks: 'Man should examine himself before he takes this Food which goes to the stomach where it is heated and digested; from there it passes through the veins into all the limbs.' Whenever we have searched our conscience and confronted it with this divine Food of which we have partaken with love and devotion, God consumes, absorbs, purifies and re-forms us; yet this only happens when we divest ourselves of our ego and allow it to be reduced to mere nothingness just as food, the longer it cooks, becomes less and less and changes its original appearance.

These, then, dear children, should be the signs by which you can tell whether God has consumed and absorbed you and whether your true being is reflected nowhere else but in him and you find nothing else but him in you. That is what our Lord meant when he said: 'Who eats my Flesh abides in me and I in him.' If you want to be purified and re-formed by him you must discard your old self because whenever a thing is to be changed into something else it must first cease to be its old self; if wood is to be changed into fire it must first lose the characteristics of wood. If you want to be absorbed into God you must first shed your ego.

Our Lord said: 'Who eats me the same shall also live by me.' My dear children, the best thing you can do to achieve this is to make full use of the Blessed Sacrament; it strips you inwardly and outwardly of your old self and reduces the old man to nothing. Just as nature changes the food and drives its invigorating force through the veins so that it becomes part of man's very existence, this divine Food withdraws you entirely from the world. Watch yourself and see whether, when you have eaten it, your heart is drawn away from everything that is not of God and whether the life which he awakened in you, flows through your veins and has its effect on your outward person, your senses, manners, words, works and way of life. This holy Sacrament disposes of everything that is evil, unnecessary and superfluous and ruthlessly casts it out so that God may come in; when he has thus entered in the form of the Food, its effect can be noticed in your whole manner of life because your love, your friendship and your thoughts are all renewed, are purer and more godly. This Sacrament also dispels man's blindness and teaches him to know himself, to turn away from himself and the world, for it is written: 'We shall be fed with the bread of life and understanding.' Whenever this sacred Food absorbs and changes man it is done so thoroughly that his whole life is regulated and formed by God. When, however, man does not sense this influence, but remains vain in his heart and full of malice, gossip and ridicule in his everyday life, when these habits become apparent in the clothes he wears, his foolishness, pastimes and love affairs, when he, though fully conscious of his undignified behaviour, yet goes to receive the Blessed Sacrament—that indeed is something which will be the cause of much sorrow. Our Lord will not absorb him into himself, just as our stomach is unwilling to keep down something unwholesome. It would be much better for this man if he did not attempt to receive Communion. Such people go to confession but they refuse to keep away from the things which cause them to commit sin. Not even the Pope can absolve us of our sins unless we are contrite and resolved to mend our ways, yet these people persist in receiving the holy Food. It would be a good thing if we had confessors who told everybody when to go to Holy Communion. There are some who might go often, others once a week, others again once in four weeks. Those who go every fourth week should, except for saying yea and nay, refrain from speaking during one week before and one week after

they have received Holy Communion, they should
also have only one meal in the morning and a bite or
two in the evening. Others receive the holy Food
only on feast days and there are some who only do
so at Easter-time; that is very little indeed, seeing
that they have the whole of Lent to prepare themselves for it. But there are people who should never
go to Holy Communion, not even if they lived a
thousand years, for one thing is certain: whosoever
is not sorry for his sins, not prepared to rectify them
and to examine his conscience, actually makes himself
guilty of doing violence to our Lord's Body, when
he receives it. Therein lies the reason why so many
people are 'infirm and weak and many sleep'.
Dear children, you do not know how worrying and
frightening all this is, or do you think it is a trifling
matter? No, indeed it is not! There are people who
want to go to Holy Communion as often as possible
during the week, not because they feel the urge but
either from force of habit or because they see others
doing it. No, children, this is not the way! Those
who want to be good and wish to protect themselves
from the occasion of sin should go reverently once a
week in order not to succumb; they should go, not
because they are so perfect but because they are so
weak.

I might tell you that if I found a man who had
led a very wicked life but had been truly and
completely converted, I would rather give him the
Body of our Lord every day for six months, than
give it once to these lukewarm people, because
I know that Holy Communion would free him
entirely from any worldliness that was still left in
him.

I have discovered what it is that makes people remain so lukewarm and insensitive, though they are aware of God, and why the Blessed Sacrament has so little effect on them. There are two reasons. The first one is that they have some hidden fault which stands in their way; it may be an inward or an outward one, it may even be that they cannot guard their tongues. Oh, children, there is no limit to the dreadful harm which arises from this habit. For God's sake, be careful or you will never succeed.

The other reason is that they go to Holy Communion by force of habit and are not driven by true love. Some habits are very good, for instance when man acquires the habit of seclusion. It is a great pity that you do not remain secluded in order to become aware of the benefit of the Food. At times it bears fruit on the third or even as late as on the fourth day if only you would watch and remain alone; but that is precisely what you refuse to do. The fruits of the Holy Sacrament cannot be born within you unless your mind is ready to receive them with love and you are withdrawn within yourself. This should be the case with everybody, everywhere and in every way because people need it and this recollection is most important; yet they remain alone as little as possible. Believe me, if you were determined to remain withdrawn, the Blessed Sacrament would bear fruit in you and through you, our Lord's nobility would become yours and you would participate in the Holy Communion of all the priests the world over. It might even happen that it would bear more fruit within you than in the priest. Man should strive after this every day while he makes his offerings, because it greatly furthers his intention to be truly converted.

May God help us that we receive the Blessed Sacrament in such a way that we are absorbed in him. Amen.

SERMON FOR THE ELEVENTH SUNDAY
AFTER PENTECOST

This is the sermon from St Mark's gospel for the eleventh Sunday and it tells how a God-loving man is not exalted by love nor driven to despair by grief; his ears are opened by the seven gifts of the Holy Ghost. (Mark, 7, 31.)

We read in to-day's gospel of the time when our Lord went from one part of the country to another and a man was brought before him who was born deaf and dumb. It is natural that when a man is deaf from birth he should also be dumb because, never having heard people speak, he does not know how to do it himself.

Our Lord put his fingers into the man's ears and, spitting, he touched his tongue, saying: 'Ephpheta,' which is: be thou opened. When the people saw what he had accomplished they came and wondered, saying: 'he has done all things well; he has made both the deaf to hear and the dumb to speak'.

Children, it is important that, first of all, we consider what it is that makes people deaf. It is because our first parents lent an ear to the whispers of the Enemy; this first deafened them and then us, so that now we cannot hear or understand the adorable language of the eternal Word, although we know that it is so intimately near to us in our innermost ground that we ourselves, our nature and thoughts, in fact everything conceivable connected

with us is not as near to us as is the eternal Word.
He never ceases to speak to us, yet we hear nothing
because of the deafness which has taken possession
of us. But whose fault is that? I shall tell you.
Something has afflicted man's ears and stopped them
up, so that he cannot hear God's loving Word any
longer; this something has also deluded man, so
that now he is dumb as well and unable to know
himself. If he wanted to speak of his inner being he
could not do so nor does he know anything about
himself or his true being. The reason for this is that
the Enemy whispered into his ear, man listened
to him and the consequence was that he became
deaf and dumb. What, then, is this dangerous
whisper of the Enemy? It consists in the disruption
of God's law and order; man is dazzled and deceived,
either by means of worldly love, his fellow-men's
opinions or the world in general and all that it stands
for, such as fortune and honour, or his own nature
with its imaginary love and favours from other
human beings. We are forced to hear the Enemy's
whisper, because he never leaves man to himself.

And mark my words, whatever it is that attracts
man—be it inwardly or outwardly, joy or grief—
the devil tampers with it, colours it with his taint
and tempts man with the faked object. The resulting
images bar the way to his inner ear, so that he
cannot hear the eternal Word. If he were to turn
away his ear and his mind it would be an easy thing
to overcome the temptation. But as soon as he lends
a willing ear and is pleased by the images, contemplating, under the devil's watchful eye, whether
or not to turn away and thereby beginning to waver,
he is almost conquered and the temptation is at

its peak. But even at this point, if he takes courage and turns away abruptly he is still able to overcome it. Then he will receive the gift of hearing the inner voice and his deafness will be conquered. This deafness, however, is not characteristic of worldly people alone, many of the clergy also suffer from it; they have turned their love and mind to the people of the world and are infatuated by them. The devil is quick to notice it and incites them to indulge in false images if he finds them so disposed. Some people are deafened because, by means of their own free will and following the example of other creatures, they find it worth while to enhance their worldly dignity. All these efforts block the way to the inner ear and consequently man can neither hear nor understand the eternal Word. Nevertheless, man must also acquire good and deeply-rooted habits —free from self-will—like prayer, meditation or others, so that his nature should be stirred, the spirit raised and he may be drawn within himself. But this should not be achieved by self-will, but rather through listening intently for the inner voice and searching for the inner ground; nor should an attempt be made to shirk the real issue, by insisting on worldly ways until one's dying days instead of going forward in search of God, but always having one's ears stopped up, so that whenever God wants to speak he cannot be heard.

Children, there are so many hindrances and the number of reluctant people is so great that it will be terrible to see the misery on the last day of Judgement, when all things will be revealed.

The word, however, is not spoken into a man's ear, unless he has a love for God. It says in the gospel:

'If you love me, you hear my word.' St Gregory said: 'Do you want to know whether you love God? Watch yourselves then, when anguish and suffering assail you spiritually—so that in your affliction you do not know which way to turn or what to do—or bodily, when excruciating pain attacks you without warning and causes great discomfort; if, in spite of this, you retain your inner peace and are not distressed nor can be induced to vent your feelings by violent words and deeds, you can be sure beyond doubt that you love God.' Where true love prevails, man is not impressed by worldly attachments nor depressed by sorrow. Whether things are given or taken away, you have inner peace as long as you have your beloved Lover. You must resign yourselves to suffering and even if you groan outwardly, you are inwardly at peace as long as you are content to do God's will and he remains with you. If, however, you are not thus disposed, you are really deaf and cannot take in the truth of the eternal Word.

You can also see whether you have the true love if you have the urge to give thanks to God for his great goodness which he shows to all his creatures in heaven and on earth and which—in his humanity—he proves through his manifold gifts and graces which he pours into mankind in a steady stream. You should prove your gratitude by loving all people, not only your own, but everybody, be they nuns, monks or anyone at all. You should have true love for them, as true as you have for yourselves and your own friends.

Believe me, dear children, this real love for the whole of mankind is immensely beneficial. You all know that it is peculiar to a genuine and serenely tranquil friend of God that his heart loves and goes out to all human beings, be they dead or alive. If it were not for these friends, we should indeed be in a sad plight.

You should also, in your outward life, let your love shine as much as possible and although you should not deprive yourselves of the necessities of life, you should nevertheless help by giving alms, comfort and advice or, if you cannot afford to give alms, at least keep your love aflame and be sure that you would be willing to give alms if you could afford them. These, then, are the real signs of love and they show that you are not deaf.

Our Lord put his fingers in the man's ear and, spitting, touched his tongue and the man spoke.

Children, the things that could be said about this miracle are wonderful, but we shall only concentrate on the seven gifts of the Holy Ghost which our Lord, by putting his fingers into the man's ears, imparted to him and by which we, too, can hear the truth.

The first gift consists in man receiving the spirit of holy fear, which frees him from his self-will and teaches him to avoid and abstain from his unruly habits and his conceit.

The second gift is that of gentleness which makes man sweet-tempered, well-disposed and merciful, so that he does not judge harshly other people's deeds and thus grows into an amiable and lovable person.

The third gift stands for wisdom, by which a man's inner being is put to the test and taught how to be at the disposal of God in order to fulfil his dearest wishes.

The fourth gift is that of divine power; man is so

filled with it, that it only seems a trifle when, either through his actions or his surrender, he has to suffer for God's sake.

The fifth is that of good counsel; those who wait for it and take it when it comes, become truly good people.

The sixth and seventh gifts point gravely in the direction of the place where understanding and discerning wisdom are to be found. These, dear children, are so sublime and noble, that it is much better to become aware of them than to express them in human language.

May God help us, that our ears be opened so that we can hear the eternal Word echoing through our souls. Amen.

SERMON FOR THE TWELFTH SUNDAY
AFTER PENTECOST

This sermon, taken from St Luke's gospel for the twelfth Sunday, teaches us to strive for God himself and to admit our own blindness and wretchedness, because this recognition will lead us to true humility, both in natural and spiritual matters. (Luke 10, 23.)

We read of the time, when, looking at those men whom his Father had entrusted to him, our Lord's Spirit rejoiced and he said: 'I thank thee, O Father, because thou hast hidden these things from the wise and prudent and hast revealed them to the little ones.' Then he turned to his beloved disciples and began to speak the words we read in the gospel appointed for this week and time of year: *Beati oculi qui vident quae vos videtis;* blessed are the eyes that see the things which you see. For I say unto you that many prophets and kings have desired to see the things that you see and have not seen them; and to hear the things that you hear and have not heard them. And behold a certain lawyer stood up, tempting him and saying: Master, what must I do to possess eternal life? But he said to him gently, yet knowing that he was at fault: What is written in the law? How readest thou? He answering, said: Thou shalt love the Lord thy God with thy whole heart, thy whole soul and thy whole mind and thy neighbour as thyself. And he said to him: This do and thou shalt live.

Let us consider the first sentence: 'Blessed are the eyes that see the things which you see.' Man has two kinds of eyes, an inner and an outer eye and were it not for the inner eye, the bodily eye would be but a contemptible thing and man nothing more than an animal.

Dear children, how is it possible that our mind—the inner eye—should be so lamentably deluded that it cannot perceive the true light? The fatal damage was done when a coarse skin, as thick as hide, was drawn over the eyes; this coarse skin has its origin either in love and attraction towards temporal things or in the man himself and all that pertains to him. It is this that made him blind and deaf, and the same applies to all men, whether they be of the clergy or the laity.

Children, what do you think is the reason that man is quite unable to come within reach of his inner ground? There are so many skins, as thick as ox-hide, and these are to be blamed; they are drawn over the inner ground and have so thoroughly overgrown its essential nature that neither God nor man can penetrate them. Do you know that some people have as many as thirty or forty such skins, thick and coarse and black as a bear's skin? But what are they? Everything you accept by way of your own will, be it wilful words and deeds, favours and disfavours, pride, self-will, pleasure in things which are not of God, hardness of heart, flippancy, careless conduct and other evils.

These and others are the things which produce the thick skins and are the obstacles which blind the eyes of man. But when he recognises his errors and is sorry for them, when he is humble and accuses himself of his guilt before God with the firm will to reform as far as possible, things will immediately change for the better because, as soon as he is prepared to confess his sins humbly, he is on the right path. But there are people who might be fast asleep for the scant notice they take of the advice given to them; their thick skins have completely overgrown their eyes and ears and they cling to their idols, whatever they may be. In fact they sit on them, just as Rachel (Sarah) did, when she took her father's idols away with her.[1] The idols' images produce the obstacles and consequently the skins cover the inner eye and ear so that the mind cannot see the road leading to bliss. 'Blessed are the eyes that see the things which you see.'

A man of sense can soon see how people with vain and worldly hearts feel completely at home with human creatures who, after all, are a mere nothing; yet this is in no way to be compared with the wonderful bliss of being at home with him who brings forth all the wonders of the world!

Our Lord said that his disciples were blessed because of what they saw. When we think this over carefully we can see that we should be blessed indeed because we see far more of our Lord Jesus Christ than the disciples did, even more than St Peter and St John. They saw that their leader was a poor, sorrowful, suffering and mortal man whereas we, in our holy and noble faith, acknowledge a great, powerful God and Lord who created heaven, earth and all the creatures out of nothing. If we see this in the proper light our eyes, even our souls, are blessed for eternity.

[1] In her flight with Jacob (Genesis 31, 34).

Dear children, the high clergy and the great masters of the Law debate about comprehension and love and which of the two is the more sublime. But we shall only deal with the Master of Life, and if we succeed in that we shall see the truth in all things. Our Lord said: 'But one thing is necessary.' What is this one thing which is so important? It is that you acknowledge your nothingness, that whatever or whoever you are or own is as nothing. Because we would not admit this one truth we inflicted such fear on our Lord that he sweated blood and because of our refusal he cried on the Cross: 'My God, why hast thou forsaken me?' Because of this one thing which was lacking he was forsaken by all men.

Dear children, if you blotted out everything you ever learned from me and other teachers and obliterated from your memory all you ever did or saw as well as all deep contemplation, and learned only how to acquire this one thing, you would have done well. That is why our Lord also said: 'Mary has chosen the best part.' It was the best of all things she could do.

Truly, if you acquired this one thing, you would not only possess one part but everything. By this I do not mean that you should be like certain people who speak glibly and humbly about their nothingness as if they had grasped the essential qualities of this virtue, but at the same time, within their souls fancy themselves to be among the greatest. These people want to appear great; but even should they deceive others, they themselves are deceived in the first place because they are the victims held fast by their own delusions.

Children, this inner ground of the soul is only

known to very few people. There may be no more than three amongst this crowd who have had some notion of it. It has nothing to do with thinking or reasoning, but it is most important that one should always have it in mind and, by perseverance, should arrive at its essential character for, as you know, continuous practice achieves in the end the perfection of our intrinsic qualities. As soon as one notices that one's inner or outer attention is drawn away, one should turn at once and sink down into the lowest abyss of the soul and quickly, without hesitation, become immersed in one's own nothingness.

Some people come to tell me that 'they do this or that deed every day, just as our Lord did' and so on and so forth. Dearest ones, if you were to imagine that your actions or your way of life are something to be proud of, it would be far better for you if you stopped all activities and turned to consider your sheer nothingness, your uselessness and impotence, instead of carrying on in your old ways and thereby forgetting your nothingness.

Let us first talk of the outward man. Look at yourselves, what you are and from whence you came. Made from an ugly, foul, evil and unclean substance, unsightly and horrible in your own and other men's eyes, what has become of you? An unclean and smelling vessel full of filth. No food or drink however clean and lovely, can be absorbed by you without it being turned immediately into nasty, evil-smelling dirt. No one is so fond of his dearest friend that, when this friend dies, he would risk the salvation of his own soul and incur eternal hell-fire so as to be able to remain with the dead body; no, he deserts him as if he were a dead dog.

God, in his turn, has set the whole of nature —like the sky, the sun and the stars—against man. Either we are freezing cold or boiling hot, frost and snow are our enemies, we feel well and then suddenly we are ill, we suffer from hunger and thirst, big animals like wolves or small ones like spiders, flies and fleas attack us and we are unable to stave them off. On the other hand, look at the dumb animals in their natural splendour. Nature supplies them with clothes which are always right whether it be cold or hot, whereas you must obtain your clothes from them. And then you fleece them and with their property you deck yourselves up, indulging in lust, comfort and pride. Is that not blindness in the highest degree? The cattle and all other animals are satisfied with the food, drink, clothes and place of rest God has provided for them, yet what fanciful measures must we adopt for the sustenance of our poor bodies!

In olden times, the saints wept when they were supposed to eat, and when they were dying they laughed.

Look again at your nothingness and wretchedness of this nature of yours. Do you like praying? Do you enjoy fasting? Do you think watching and kneeling are pleasant? What is the answer to all these questions? 'For the good which I will, I do not, but the evil which I will not, that I do.' Look at the manifold and unbelievable temptations which assail you and the inward and outward ailments which God inflicts on you! Be sure to learn the one, necessary thing and be of good hope! God sends you all these impediments for your own good; they should make you recede into your nothingness which will bring you much more benefit than if you were highly respected by men. Then be prepared, for people will attack you with cruel words and threaten you and the influential as well as the reasoning people will argue against you with high-sounding words, as if they were the apostles come to life. Dearest ones, sink deep down into your inner ground, your nothingness and let the whole Tower of Babel crash down on you with all the devils hell can hold and all the creatures in heaven and on earth. All this will serve you well. Sink down then, and you will partake of the best.

People say: 'Lord, Lord, I think every day about Jesus Christ's suffering, how he stood before Pilate, before Herod, at the pillar' and so it goes on.

Dear children, listen to my words: contemplate our Lord not so much as the perfect man, but concentrate on the all-powerful, almighty and eternal God, who created and can undo heaven and earth by uttering one single word and who, though he is above all beings and beyond comprehension, willed to be crucified for the sake of his poor creatures. Shame on you, mortal vermin that you ever thought of your own honour, pride and gain! Go and surrender to the Cross from wherever it may come, whether it be a spiritual or a bodily one! Let your proud mind bow down under his crown of thorns and follow your crucified God, with your mind and your selves humiliated in every possible way, since it was almighty God who was persecuted and condemned by his creatures and who died for them on the Cross.

That is how you ought to mould your mind and imitate his patient suffering and humility, not as those do who, though each one of them thinks of the sacred Passion of our Lord, are dulled, blind and uncouth in their love; the thought of him does not influence their spiritual exercises in such a way as to make them give up their comfort, pride, honour and sensual gratifications; on the contrary, they remain exactly as they were before.

Oh, how little fruition the loving Passion of our Lord brings to these people! The fruits of men's love for him are always apparent in their imitation of his Passion, the way they live, behave and work.

Dear children, thus you should imitate and contemplate our Lord's suffering, so that it may come to life within you. Abase yourselves to nothing, accept it as unjust that the earth carries you on its shoulders instead of opening and swallowing you up, and think of the many thousands of souls in hell, who perhaps never had as many bad habits as you indulge in and, had God but given them as much light and as many favours as he has granted you, might have made much better use of them. But he spared you and waits, whereas he condemned the others for eternity. Bear this in mind; even when you only take a drop of water, do not do it in a spirit of arrogance as if it were your due, but accept it in humble fear. Use all things only as far as you need them to sustain your body and not for your gratification. Some people talk about great, wise, supernatural and transfigurate things as if they had been lifted into the heaven of heavens yet they have never even taken the first step towards looking at themselves and acknowledging their own nothingness. They may have arrived at the recognition of rational truths, but the living truth, the one Truth can only be found if we follow the path which leads across our nothingness, and whosoever has not gone that way will have to bear the loss and be exposed to great shame on the day when all things shall be revealed. O children, that is when these people will wish that they had never either pretended to be holy nor heard or spoken about deep rational problems or acquired a great name, but had rather spent their lives in tilling their land, taking their cattle to pasture and earning their living by the sweat of their brow.

The day will come when God will call us to account for all the lovely gifts he distributes so generously and which are abused in such a way that they can bear no fruit.

As for self abasement, that should not result in a fear born from doubts as is the sceptics' wont, but in a humble and tranquil submission to God and his creatures.

Should a man discern something in himself and take it to be humility, he is undoubtedly wrong. That is why our Lord said: 'Unless you become as little children you cannot enter the Kingdom of Heaven.' Therefore we should attach no importance to anything. Our Lord also said: 'Let the little ones come to me.' The earth is the lowest among the four elements and, in its lowliness, has fled furthest away from heaven with the result that heaven pursues it with all its strength and the help of the sun, the moon and the stars and that these bring forth the best fruit from the earth. By the same token, the deeper the vale, the more abundant the water, as also the valleys are much more fertile than the mountains.

Children, this true self-abasement sinks down into the innermost divine abyss and loses itself entirely, being truly lost to the world and self. *Abyssus, abyssum invocat*, 'deep calleth upon deep.' By virtue of its depth and its cognition of self-annihilation, the created abyss merges into the non-created, infinite Abyss, so that they unite, the Nothing and the nothingness becoming one.

That is the Nothing of which St Dionysius spoke, when he said that God is none of the things which man can express, understand, or perceive. That is the moment when the human spirit is wholly resigned, so much so that if God wanted to annihilate him and totally absorb him in the Nothing, his love would answer the call and make him submerge in it, because he knows, loves and enjoys nothing except the One.

Children, the eyes which have thus learned to see are indeed blessed and our Lord could well say: 'Blessed are the eyes that see the things which you see.'

May God help us to become blessed through the true vision of our nothingness. Amen.

SERMON FOR THE FEAST OF THE ASSUMPTION OF OUR LADY

This is the sermon which speaks about the end of our Lady's life and how she was taken up into Heaven; it shows how we ought not to settle down to enjoy bodily or spiritual things, but should search for our undiscernible God and live in his inheritance and that of wisdom. (Eccl. 24, 7.)

These words were spoken by a wise man and we read that our Lady also said: 'I have sought rest in all things and shall abide in the inheritance of the Lord.' Those words are well attributed to our Lady, because for as long as she, by her power, 'compassed the circuit of heaven, penetrated into the bottom of the deep, walked in the waves of the sea and stood in all the earth' she could find no rest.

Dear children, instead of trying to tune up your spiritual exercises to a very high pitch, spend one hour in offering a special devotion to our most loving Lady, asking her to help us to draw and lead us to her beloved Child.

Dearest ones, her excellence is beyond all human conception. The wondrous awe of carrying her God and Creator first in her womb and then in her arms, of being in his presence in a way too blissful to be grasped by the senses, never for one moment doubting his divinity and being able to be quite at her ease with him! Although he lived with her as her Child, she never indulged in self-love but was for ever immersed and overflowing into the divine abyss where she found peace, her home, her rest and her inheritance.

Children, the poison of the Fall has dragged human nature down to its lowest level. Man is a created being and stands between the two terms of time and eternity. Time should be nothing more to us than a transition on our way towards the end —eternity—where we should find our abode. But such are the consequences of the Fall that man in his wretched blindness gets hold of the worst of everything and thereby not only loses his peace of mind but also loses sight of his true aim. As soon as nature has too many attachments it cleaves to whatever it comes into contact with—be it spiritual or bodily, inward or outward—and wishes to abide there. The way in which the people of the world seek their peace and pleasures is all too obvious; they will find out later on in what a sad plight they are, particularly those who harbour a worldly heart beneath a clerical garb and find their rest in temporal things. Their state is indeed a precarious one and if they knew just how precarious it is, their hearts would be filled with anguish.

You know as well as I do that God made all things for our use and sustenance and not for the sake of our gratification.

Children, I tell you the following because I love you. I have been falsely accused of having said that unless people promise to do what I tell them, I shall refuse to hear their confession. It would be entirely wrong to say: 'do what *I* want you to do,' because I want everybody to act according to the law and I do not expect anybody's promise on that issue. I can absolve nobody—not even the Pope—unless he is sorry for his sins and has the firm will not only to avoid the sins but also the occasion to sin.

There are people, however, who, though they deliberately cling to the things which are the causes of their sins, go to confession and receive the Body of our Lord, whilst all the time they refuse to admit their sin. So long as they do not steal and are not guilty of gross impurity they continue in this vein. It remains to be seen what chances they have of obtaining their final absolution and no doubt in the end they will feel the bitter sting of remorse. They turn away from God and look for their peace and pleasures in men, dress, food or comforting creatures, sometimes even in things which may seem good at first glance. When they have committed a sin, they hurry to outward confession before they have inwardly confessed to God, humbly acknowledging their guilt. This outward confession, however, only helps to appease nature and to silence the inner reproaches and chastisement, because as soon as the people have confessed their sins, the reproaches cease and they are at peace. True confession and the inner chastisement are just like an open wound, which hurts and bleeds and thus rids itself of the poison of sins.

The natural man, too, seeks rest in spiritual exercises and some people even perform them by way of good intentions and by practising seclusion, but they are so intent on these things that—though good in themselves—they bar the way to God, the eternal Truth.

Children, what I want to impress on you is, in short, that whenever man seeks rest in something which is not purely and simply God, he must needs find it to be corrupt. No, indeed, the achievement of perfection does not depend on whether your appearance is shabby and someone else's is elegant; you need more than that.

Some people tell me how well they succeeded with such lovely and pure activities as prayer, vigil, fasting or weeping and how easy it was; yet I can see that they failed. Do not forget that however good a thing may be or may seem to be, however free from images, forms or visions—attained with the help of reason or otherwise—as soon as man claims it as his own in order to rejoice and rest in it, he has already sown the seed of corruption. Only when one denies oneself and every attribute to one's person, can one become totally immersed in the hidden and ineffable good, which is God; St Dionysius tells us how to achieve this aim when he says: 'Everybody ought to be ever mindful of his nothingness by knowing nothing, grasping nothing and thereby wanting nothing else but their self-denial; seek nothing for yourselves and receive everything by sinking into the Nothing. For God is none of the things you can name; he is more than wise, more than essential, more than good, yet none of the terms applied to him can describe how infinitely far he stands above them, nor can human understanding, however deep it is, ever come within reach of him.

Dear children, commit your inner peace into the hands of the indiscernible God and seek neither perception nor enlightenment. Do as a well-trained dog does when he finds a nice piece of meat: he does not touch it, but flees from it, because many hard blows have taught him to behave in this way. You, too, will reap the benefit if you hold on humbly to your nothingness which, after all, is what you really are. If something exists in a certain place, it is his, not yours; avoid becoming engrossed in any other matter, however real it may seem, even if it is free of form, images and visions and is supernatural.

'Father,' some people say to me, 'it was all so evident and clear, that it must have been sent by God.' Dear children, leave actual things well alone and don't turn to them when you are in search of inner peace, don't ask questions or try to increase your learning, but rather remain in the depth and sink further into your ignorance and disregard of human wisdom, and, by means of your poverty be true to your hidden and secret God. Don't imagine that you, a mere human being, can ever comprehend the great, hidden and secret God; renounce all perception and enlightenment and find your rest and abode in him. We read in the book of the prophet Ezechiel the following words: 'In the day that they go into the sanctuary, into the inner court, to minister unto me, they shall have no inheritance, for I am their inheritance.' Although this only refers to priests, it really applies to all spiritually minded people who wish to enter the 'inner court' or, in other words, the obscurity of God's secret; their inheritance is to be no more and no less than the divine, formless, nameless, invisible and secret Essence and therein they shall have their inheritance. They are to pay no attention—inwardly or outwardly —to material things lest they become corrupt, nor to their outward appearance, for a smooth surface is often merely for show. It is far better for them to love the rough and uneven and keep away from all pleasant feelings and sensations. Dear children, do not give in, but continue to seek your nothingness. When God created all things he was faced with the sheer void; he did not form things from something else but made them from nothing. God can only dwell and work in the nothingness, and your response to his work is most intense when you suffer in order to be nothing. If you want always to be ready to receive his gifts and the deeds with which he endows the very being of his best friends, you must first of all endeavour to annihilate yourselves in your inner ground, because it is primarily selfishness and the urge for comfort which hinder God in doing his noble work in our souls.

Job, that holy and wise man, whom God praised and of whom he said that he was just and simple and that his equal could not be found, said one day: 'All that I have shall go down into the deepest pit; thinkest thou that there at least I shall have rest?' Children, by speaking of 'all that he has', this holy man did not think of the nothing from which he was created (for in this respect all men are alike) but of his nothingness resulting from his sins. Because of his knowledge of guilt this just man was prepared to descend into the lowest depth, the darkest and most painful recess of hell and wondered whether he was called to atone for our fallen nature and accumulated guilt. He was ready to bear all these acute sufferings and never to emerge again— although who knows whether he was not in some way satisfied that he was guilty of these our deliberate sins?

A similar thing happened to one of our brothers

whose name was Wigman. He was so filled with the knowledge of his guilt that he could find no resting-place except in the lowest depth of hell, below Lucifer. While he was there, he heard a voice calling from heaven: 'Wigman, make haste and come unto the highest throne, into your Father's heart.'

St Gregory said: 'These people seek death, but they do not find it.' This love in its abysmal abnega-tion finds its response in the life of God's truth, for the very reason that it did not seek, desire or intend it. Thus, dear children, you can see that the lower you go the higher you are raised, and the less you are the more you receive.

Now for the words which our Lady spoke: 'I have sought rest and shall abide in the inheritance of the Lord.' We have two types of inheritance in which we ought to live.

The first one is temporal, the noble life, Passion and sacred countenance of our Lord and into this we should immediately enter. The other one awaits us and is the glorified inheritance of the blessed divinity. It is the inheritance which was promised to us, which we will share with him when we are of his household for all eternity. In the same measure as we make the temporal inheritance—the life of our Lord—faithfully our own by loving him and being genuinely grateful to him, we shall come into the eternal inheritance.

Dear children, the wounds of our Lord have all healed, except for the five sacred wounds which will remain open until the last day of Judgement. As for the divine splendour which shines forth from them and the bliss which the saints obtain from them —these are beyond human comprehension.

These five wounds or gates, as it were, are to be our inheritance while on earth and we are to pass through them in order to enter into the eternal inheritance of our Father's kingdom. The Holy Ghost keeps watch at the gates and his great love is always ready to admit us, whenever we knock, in order to let us enter into our Father's inheritance, because you can be quite certain that whosoever enters through these gates cannot go astray.

Children, the five wounds are to teach us five lessons which in their turn lead us directly to him. They are seclusion, suffering, silence, self-disdain, self-denial and true tranquillity. Embrace the wound of the left foot and receive from it the strength to avoid all pleasure and satisfaction which is not sent by God. From the wound in the right foot learn how to suffer whatever befalls your inner or outer selves, wherever it comes from. The wound in his left hand shall teach you to keep inner and outward silence, for whosoever possesses the virtue of keeping his peace cannot go wrong. The wound of the right hand is to fill you with disdain, or in other words, make you spiritually and bodily indifferent to temporal things, coincidences and passing thoughts, and free you from the images which might stand in the way of your love and respect for him. Forgo all these occasional things, be free of them and let your true being slip into his adorable and loving heart, into the glorious bridal chamber which he has opened for his own who are willing to give him their heart; there he will fold you in his loving arms and there you will be for all eternity. This is the moment when you must learn to deny yourselves in every way, in loving, suffering, possessing, desiring, in time and eternity, so that his will and divine heart can take up their abode in you and in all his creatures. Discard all other things and let him be the sole resident.

Dear children, if in this way and through other holy devotions you make this temporal inheritance your own, you will surely enter through the gates into the eternal inheritance. Offer up to the heavenly Father our Lord's innocent suffering for your deserved suffering, his innocent mind for your guilty mind, his sacred words for your unholy words and all his actions, his humility, patience, meekness and love for all the things which you lack. As soon as you have entered into this inheritance to the best of your abilities, you may firmly depend upon your coming into the inheritance of the life to come, where you will be at home and rest, sharing it with our Lord and our Lady.

Let us then ask God to help us to seek rest in all things, so that we may come at last into the eternal inheritance. Amen.

SERMON FOR THE FEAST OF THE NATIVITY OF THE BLESSED VIRGIN MARY

Come over to me, all ye that desire me and be filled with my fruits. (*Eccl.* 24, 26.)

To-day we celebrate the joyful day when the holy Virgin, our Lady, was born, pure and immaculate, from her mother's womb, wherein she had been sanctified. She was the instrument by which we regained what we had lost in Paradise—the noble image which the Father had fashioned after his likeness—and which was destroyed through sin. She was, together with the Father, to regenerate all the members of the Body and bring them back to their origin, while God, in his unfathomable mercy, through her agency was ready to lend us a helping hand—if we were willing to take it—to raise us from the pit into which we had fallen.

We read the following words referring to the Virgin in the book of Wisdom: 'Come over to me, all ye that desire me and be filled with my fruits.' These words are definitely to be attributed to the heavenly Father and they lead and draw us to contemplate him as the Creator, but at the same time they were also spoken with regard to the Virgin, as her birth falls within the Father's plan of procreation and they are to guide us so that we merge into and are inspired by the adorable birth. The holy Virgin said: 'All who have a great longing for me and for this birth will at times be able to look upon me.' Thus our longing is further increased or, as St Augustine said: 'Lord, you have made us for you and therefore our hearts never rest, unless they are at peace with you.' This restless longing which should always be within us, is disturbed and interfered with by hostile forces born in us such as temporal, transient, sensual things — friendship, society, dress, food, in short everything which makes for the satisfaction and pleasure of human beings and fills them with worldly joy. While you deliberately allow these detrimental pleasures to take possession of you—even if their hold on you is only slight—God will not place his seed in your being. The smallest infatuation deprives you of your omnipotent God and of the lovely birth he wants to effect in you; it also smothers the longing you should have for him, it kills the comfort this birth would bring you, and yet it is just these petty desires which are in his way. When people complain and say: 'I have no love and feel no longing,' it is only because these obstacles hinder their progress and check the love and the longing. Search yourselves and see what the obstacle may be, because, after all, you know best. Do not ask me, but ask yourselves why you have neither love nor longing. You obviously want to enjoy God as well as the world, and that is impossible; you cannot have joy in God and in the world, however hard you may try.

I am now speaking not of necessities, of the things we have through or in God nor of those without which nature cannot exist, nor of the joy of eating when one

is hungry, the joy of drinking when one is thirsty
or the relief of resting and going to sleep when one
is weary. When, however, these things are done,
not so much because nature demands them but for
the sheer pleasure and gratification derived from
them, you oust God from your being, although, to
be sure, there are many more harmful pleasures
than these and the obstacles are accordingly greater.
But we must remember that it is not always possible
to distinguish between the necessity demanded by
nature and the pleasure one feels while satisfying
this necessity. On the other hand, if man does not
want to thwart the eternal birth but wishes to
increase his longing for God, he must be able to
master these pleasures of the senses, of nature and
of human creatures, because the less he indulges in
them, the more he will be ready to partake of the
others, for in the same measure as the callousness
produced by natural desires is disposed of, the warm
glow of divine love can take its place. It is also
imperative that man should not remain a captive
to his own comfort and habits and thus be kept in
the dark recesses of his fallen nature. Some people
behave as if they were blind and whatever they do
is done blindly, unreasonably and without fore-
thought. And believe me, your confessor has no
power over these vices—your excesses and selfishness—as long as you have the intention to adhere to
them; even if you confessed them ten times a day
it would be of no use unless you were willing to
break with them. And remember, if you consciously
give way to your infatuation towards created beings,
you will never come into God's presence. It can be
read in holy Scripture and the gospels over and over

again and it is the law of the Old as well as of the
New Testament. It reads: 'Thou shalt love the
Lord, thy God.' We also read: 'He that does not
leave everything behind is not worthy of me' and
again: 'Not everyone that saith to me, Lord, Lord,
shall enter into the kingdom of heaven, but he that
doeth the will of my Father who is in heaven, he
shall enter into the kingdom of heaven.' Do you
really think God wants to share his kingdom with
these wretched people who cling to their sins and that
it was for them that he shed his blood and gave his
life? Be careful and do not imagine that he is so
easily appeased; his wrath will descend on the
sinners and if you knew its magnitude you would
shrink with terror. He gave us all things so that they
may lead us back to him and he is to be our only
aim. Do you think I am joking? No, indeed, neither
does your holy order make a saint of you, nor do my
cowl, my tonsure, my cloister or my saintly brothers
make a saint of me. I must have a holy, immaculately
pure inner ground without attachments if I want to
become a saint. It is no good if I keep on repeating
'Lord, Lord,' if I pray, study, use fine language and
impress the people by my wisdom—no, no, this is
not all that is needed, there is much more to it than
that. If you want to cheat yourselves it will hurt you,
not me. Look at your worldly hearts and minds,
your vanity in spite of your clerical garb. These
poisons probe deeply into your very being and are
like a tree on to which a shoot from an alien plant
has been grafted, which sends its sap to the tree's
roots and produces fruit of the grafted shoot's kind
and not the fruit of the tree. In the same way these
outward and alien influences under which you have

fallen will bear the fruit in you which they have conceived.

Also your good works which ought to be performed for the glory of God will be controlled by creatures and will therefore be useless; in short, all your inward and outward forces will be dominated by this alien sap. Job said: 'In the horror of a vision by night when deep sleep is wont to hold men, fear seized upon me and trembling, and all my bones were affrighted. And when a spirit passed before me, the hair of my flesh stood up. There stood one whose countenance I knew not, an image before my eyes.'

The horror of nocturnal visions is the dark and blinding dread of being the slave of one's possessions and it is followed by such great fear as to make one tremble all over. The spirit which passed before him was God, who passed by.

Holy Scripture, too, speaks to-day of a transit— a passage. The word '*transire*' is used twice and stands for two passages. The first one is the Spirit of God passing before and moving towards us, the second one occurs when our spirit moves towards God. As you have heard, an ingress must be preceded by an egress, because, as the masters tell us, one thing cannot have two forms; the wood must perish, so that the fire can blaze, the core must die so that the tree may grow and, by the same token, if God wants to bring to pass his birth in us, our natural selves must die.

St Gregory also mentioned that the hair of his flesh stood up when the Spirit passed before him. If you think of the hair and how it has its roots in the flesh, you can compare it with the fibres which tie human beings to their old habits and which must be shaven off with the sharp razor of holy fervour. The razor must be sharpened by God's all-powerful and hidden judgement and his consuming justice which does not let one single thought go by without testing it; as for the smallest image to which the will still clings, that also must be consumed by the searing fires of Purgatory before man can appear before God.

But no sooner has the hair been cropped than it grows again and one must apply the sharp razor with renewed fervour. Some people are so zealous that as soon as they detect a single distracting thought they attack it and reject it with an iron will-power. At first it seems a great effort to be always watching oneself, but once one has acquired the habit it comes quite easily and what at first needed an iron will can then be disposed of with the flick of a finger.

Man should be filled with active love for mankind, not only for special and respectable people, but for everybody, including the common people and the poor. Such was the love of our Lady's father and mother—St Joachim and St Ann—that they divided all they had into three equal parts. One part was reserved for the service of God and the Temple. The second part was given to the poor and the third part they used for themselves. Wherever greed and stinginess are admitted into our being, they surround their victim with an unclean, coarse and evil fence. But man should be gentle and stand above such despicable and transient things, for whosoever gives will receive, whosoever forgives will be forgiven and you will be measured according to what you have meted out.

However, there are people who cling to spiritual things; it is, as it were, as if hair were growing inwards which cannot therefore be detected, yet might be the very thing which hinders them from ever coming into God's presence. Such people might well have lived very pure lives and practised great mortification while, unknown to them, this clinging thing might lie hidden in their inner ground. For those, then, who wish to live for the truth it would be very beneficial if they had a friend of God to whom they could go for spiritual advice and who would direct them according to the Holy Ghost. Unless one is closely acquainted with these people it is very difficult to detect their adherence to things, but they themselves should seek out an experienced friend of God who can show them the right path even if it means walking as much as a hundred miles. An ordinary confessor, however indifferent and uneducated a man he may be, will also be of help, as the Holy Ghost speaks through him by virtue of his ministry so that at times he himself does not understand what he is saying. People should submit to their confessor's judgement and follow his advice, instead of depending on their own interpretations.

The holy Virgin is a perfect example. When a child, she obeyed her elders, her father and mother, after which she was placed under the supervision of the priest at the Temple. Later she was under the protection of St Joseph, then our Lord Jesus Christ took care of her and finally St John took her unto him, as our Lord commanded him.

And thus we should ask her devoutly to take

charge of us and as this is her birthday—to help us
to be reborn into the eternal Source. May God help
us to achieve this. Amen.

SERMON FOR THE FEAST OF THE EXALTATION OF THE HOLY CROSS

This is the day of the raising up of the Holy Cross from which the Redeemer of the world hung, for the sake of love. The Cross should enable us to be re-born into the nobility to which eternity had pre-destined us; the love of the Cross is to effect our re-admission. (John 12, 31.)

It is a sheer impossibility to express in human language the supreme grandeur of the Cross. Our Lord said: 'And I, if I be lifted up from the earth, will draw all things to myself.' By this statement he meant that he would draw and raise unto himself our human hearts, our joy and pleasure in worldly things as well as our proud, complacent minds which cling so fondly to the temporal gratification of the senses. All this he wants to draw unto him so that he should stand above all our desires and reign supreme in our hearts, because once man has become conscious of God's greatness all worldly and finite things seem as nothing to him.

This Cross of love, which is Christ crucified, transcends all saints and angels and all their joy and bliss; in addition, in the same degree as his Essence abides on the highest peak of perfection, so he wants to dwell on the highest attainable pinnacle of our human nature, where the truest, the most intense and perceptive love and mind are to be found. He wants to lift the lowest forces to the level of the highest and absorb them one and all in his Person. If we let him have his way he will draw us into his height of perfection and into the very end of all things. But it is imperative that if we wish to arrive and remain there, we must admit him into our being. As much as I give him, he will give me and that is only fair.

But, oh, how this loving Cross is being neglected and how barred it is from the inner being by a leaning towards creatures which is, alas, in these our critical times, a prevalent vice among clerics and others alike and results in the eternal loss of hearts and human beings.

Children, it is a most deplorable thing when the human heart and senses fall prey to this vice and if only one knew the effects of such an attitude, one would shrink in terror from God's anger and revenge. Yet, not only do these people persist in and suffer this vice to spread as if it were a pastime—whereas it is become a habit—but they also approve of it and pretend that it is honourable—whereas it is a mockery, which would make the saints shed tears of blood. Our Lord's wounds, inflicted for the sake of love, are again torn open by the grief he feels when he sees that the hearts for which he gave his young life and loving, holy soul are brazenly snatched away from him and that he is expelled from them and slandered. That is a cause for shame and must move God to pity.

Children, do not believe these things just because I say so. No, the holy gospel is full of them. We read: 'No man can serve two masters, for he will love the one and hate the other'; again it says: 'If thy right eye scandalise thee, pluck it out and cast it from thee,' and again: 'For where thy treasure is there is thy heart also.'

Now, children, examine yourselves and see how much of your heart is devoted to God and whether he is your dearest treasure. St Augustine said: 'If you love the world, you are of the world, for the soul would rather be where it loves than where it merely gives life,' and St Paul wrote: 'If I speak with the tongues of angels, if I distribute all my goods to feed the poor, if I deliver my body to be burned and have no love, I am nothing.'

Well then, my dear sisters, you should be active in love and accept with deep gratitude the eminent grace which God in his love has bestowed upon your order in the form of our Lord's Body. From the bottom of my heart I request of you that, while you live in these troublesome times, your devotion should not slacken or, even worse, die out altogether. Human nature is not as steadfast as it was of old and unless we hold on to God with our whole strength we must needs succumb.

Things were altogether different in olden times, but nowadays men are in dire need of a powerful support if they are to be saved from coming to grief. And do not imagine that this support is to be sought after as if one were on the way to perfection; it is simply needed because human nature is so sick and failing (it is the sick who need the physician, not those in good health), and the help and strength are to protect and keep men from that grievous fall under which many clerical men of to-day are labouring. That is why one ought not even to venture a discussion as to whether or not they attain to great perfection or perform good deeds. It suffices if they are willing to keep the rules of their holy order as far as possible, to have at least the good intention to do so, or, if they are unable to fulfil them, to obtain permission from their superiors to abstain from them. One does not need much sense to achieve this, the main thing is that one has the will to do the right and proper thing and that, as far as possible, one's eyes may be opened to the deadly cancer from which one is suffering and that one may remain alert to the danger. That is the reason that our dear younger sisters should frequently and ardently receive the sacred Body of our Lord.

But now I want to plead for and defend our dear elder sisters. They were active and filled with sanctity at a time when humanity was not in such a sad plight as it is to-day and thus they were extremely severe in the execution of their order's rules. And because they loved and held on to these rules they also kept them and, according to the old customs, went once in every fortnight to receive the Body of our Lord. Their great perfection and sanctity warranted that they needed no more; things were better and sounder then than they are nowadays when nature in young people has been corrupted and they have much less power of resistance than they had of old. That is why they are in need of more help, because without a specially firm support they cannot attain to the highest mode of living. Everything in their nature tends to sink into the sensual regions of carnal desires. Therefore I beg of you, do not seek the company of those who live after that fashion, nor of those, whose youth, sickness of mind and kindred mentality makes them well disposed towards that sort of life. This is also the reason, my dear sisters and dearly beloved children, that I do not ask great perfection or sanctity of you as long as you have a great love for your holy order, the intention to keep its rules—dictated by love—as best you can, are prepared to keep quiet in all the places where silence is required, particularly at table and in choir and are on your guard against familiarity with people who could estrange you from God. The old sisters avoid these people by means of their sanctity and the young should do so because of their sickness. Rest assured that if you steadily pursue this course, God will befriend you and you will be free from the evil cause which does the damage and deadens the hearts of men. Do you realise how many convents have been made to endure unbearable sufferings? Had it not been that they persevered as ardently with their wonderful devotions as had always been their wont, they would not have survived.

Dear children, be not alarmed if you feel no sweetness in your devotion. When man is doing what he is asked to do, yet his inner being seems utterly forsaken, when he braces his whole strength to focus it on God and yet remains calm, when he longs for a sensitive love for God, yet his heart contracts like a dark, hard and insensible crust— then suffering exceeds all human perceptions and feelings. This cross, dear children, surpasses all the crosses that man can suffer and the bitter desolation of it drives him deeper into the ground of the living truth than all the feelings taken together.

Our Lord said: 'My God, why hast thou forsaken me?' Yet on Mount Olivet he said: 'Thy will, not mine, be done.'

Children, be not afraid, for our Lord also said: 'If any man will come after me, let him deny himself and take up his cross and follow me.' This cross is Christ crucified who shall and must be reborn in us with the help of our natural and spiritual forces: our reason, our will, our outward being, our senses and particularly the following four forces.

The first one is our worldly pleasure, which must be pierced by the birth of the Cross. St Paul said: 'And they that are Christ's have crucified their flesh with the vices and concupiscences.' These must be curbed and restrained.

The second force must control our anger so that we remain calm and are convinced that the other person's view is more correct than our own; it must teach us to avoid quarrels and squabbles and to be passive, quiet and really good in every respect, whichever way the wind may blow.

One of you, for instance, may be attending a meeting where a few people chatter incessantly without ever stopping. Dear children, that is the moment when you should learn to be calm, to suffer and to withdraw into yourselves.

Can you imagine that a man should love an art and refuse to learn more about it? If, for instance, he wanted to become a fencing-master and would not learn the art of fencing, he might do great damage if he began to fence without any knowledge and skill. In the same manner we should learn how best to fight any adversities that come our way.

The other two forces which must be pierced by the birth of the cross are of a more subtle kind; they are our reason and our spiritual appetites. To sum up, the most loving Christ crucified must be born in our inward and outward being, in our body and our mind. Thus we shall be born again into him by the consummation of his Spirit, as is written in the holy gospel: 'You shall become as little children'.

Dear children, if you live in this manner, you will feel as if you were in heaven and all your sins will be forgiven you through the birth of this holy Cross within you.

May God help us so to cling to Christ, the loving Cross that without intermission it may be newly born in us. Amen.

A SERMON GIVING GOOD ADVICE AND OFFERING HOLY GUIDANCE

Dear children, I would advise, exhort and beg of you that you learn how to confess from your pure and innermost heart, all your sins to God and how to be deeply aware of your guilt, weighing up in your mind your sorrow against your great sins. Do not make a point of making a long and merely outward confession, talking much yet only repeating your daily shortcomings in so many different words. Surely, children, that can be of little profit to you, whereas it wastes the precious time of the confessor and makes him feel vexed and uneasy.

Believe me, you cannot rid yourselves of your sins by talking a lot about them and, as I have told you time and again: neither confessor nor priest has power over the sins. Turn towards your inner selves for, unless you labour under a mortal sin, the outward repetition without inward communion bears little fruit. It only proves that the person concerned is slack in examining her conscience because, if the inner truth prevails, daily incidents whether large or small are so completely blotted out that they are hardly noticed. If inward confession with God were thus achieved, it would yield good results. But of course I only speak of daily offences and God preserve you from mortal sins.

Dear children, it is of the utmost importance that

man should become aware of his inner self. A number of thick skins has overgrown and is now covering the ground of man's soul, so that he is barred from seeing and perceiving the truth, and though he knows a quantity of other things, he cannot know himself. Thirty or forty of these skins, thick and hard as the hide of an ox conceal the soul from him and he resembles a tan-pit where the skins are turning sour from the tannic acid and lie one on top of the other from the ground upwards. How do you imagine that the state of such a soul can be set right by confession? But what exactly are those hides? They are all the things which concern you and your possessions, the way you love, care for, seek and use them, but which, in relation to God, constitute no reality or true aim. They are all idols of the natural order and are made up of such things as outward appearances, selfish pleasures, wilfulness or gratification of the senses. Man is possessed of them, just as Sarah (Rachel) was, when she sat upon her father's idols, and the result of this slackness in the face of divine things is that such people are restless, negligent and arrogant. These, then are the hides and, though they are not a matter for confession, man should look them squarely in the face, humbly confess them to God and throw himself at his feet. When man thus admits his guilt and, with the help of the Lord, endeavours to turn away from his faults as far as possible, all will be well with him.

A SERMON ON HOW ONE SHOULD MAKE A SHORT CONFESSION

The following opening words may be used when making a short confession of everyday offences in one's own religious community:

'I confess to being guilty of having sinned by yielding to vain and useless reflections even during the hours of prayer when good thoughts should have been uppermost in my mind. My slackness is responsible for this offence. I have also given way to unnecessary and unprofitable talk, breaking the silence in places and at times when speaking was not permitted; I spoke in a rash, vain, hard, foolish, sarcastic and inconsiderate way, insinuating and hinting at ugly and mischievous things. I also sinned in works, by being slack in myself, in the service of God, my order, choir and rules, by lacking in obedience and gratitude inasmuch as I did not love or give praise to God, nor heed his exhortations, and in this way, because I did not keep the rules of poverty, chastity and obedience as well as all other things which I had promised to God and to my order, I did not show my sisters the good example they should have seen in me. I confess to being guilty of all these sins.'

Thus you may crave God's pardon, thinking or saying to him: 'Dear Lord, if I could obtain your pardon and if I were allowed to move freely, I would go in search of it and get it, even if it meant swimming across the Rhine or trudging through snow, sleet and rain. Dearest Father, as I can now do no more I come to ask you to grant me of your charity, the absolution for my sins and a share in all the wholesome practices performed in this and all the other churches. And I ask of you, by the love of your bleeding wounds from whence all grace flows, to absolve me of my sins.

You ought to be able to comfort the whole world by the faith and utter trust which you put into your words.

A SERMON AND A PROFITABLE LESSON ON GOD IN HIS ONENESS

Moses spoke thus: 'Hear, O Israel, the Lord our God is one Lord.' We can greatly profit from the special, intrinsic and various qualities which we attribute to him and from his Essence, when we contrast it with our nothingness. Although—as I have told you many a time—before the coming of Christ man only thought in terms of time, the event of our Lord's birth, life, works and way of life, should teach man how to lift up his mind and let it soar from temporal to eternal conceptions.

Man is able to mirror his mind in God's qualities if he perceives that God is pure Essence, Being of all beings and yet none of all these attributes. Everything that exists, that is a being, that has being and is good, is of God.

St Augustine said: 'When you see a good man, a good angel or even the heavenly good and take away the man, the angel and heaven, you are left with the essence of goodness, which is God. For he is in all things and yet infinitely far above them.' While all created beings may *have* goodness or love, they *are* not goodness or love, God alone is the Essence of goodness, of love and of everything which we know to have an essence. In the light of all this, man should take a look at himself, sink down into the Essence, using his whole strength of

purpose in order to be truly and completely
immersed in the contemplation of God's Essence,
his nothingness being absorbed, renewed and filled
with it, the Essence which alone *is*, and *lives* and
works in all things. Furthermore man should consider
the quality, the united Oneness of God's Being, as
he is ultimately the single One in whom all manifold-
ness is united, single and one in his Essence. It is
reflected in his actions, his wisdom, his rewards,
his love, his ordering, mercy and justice. Go then
and offer him your inconceivable diversities, that
they may be absorbed in his Oneness.

Man should also be conscious of God's inexpressible seclusion. Moses said: 'Verily thou art a hidden
God.' He is far deeper hidden in all things than the
pith of the soul is hidden from man. He is utterly
hidden in the ground of truth, incomprehensible to
man. That is wherein you should penetrate, using
your entire strength to leave far behind every
thought of your worldliness, which is as remote and
alien to the inner self as only an animal can be,
living, as it does, without knowledge, perception or
awareness of anything except its senses. Sink down
and hide in the seclusion from all worldly influences,
from everything foreign and not attuned to the
Essence of all things. But this is not meant to be
said for the sake of mere metaphors and mental
reflections, it should be done really and truly,
stretching your will to the utmost and longing to
rise above the senses. Then man may witness the
uniqueness of divine solitude within a silent seclusion
where never a word is spoken——the essential meaning
of the Word is not put into language——nor one
single action performed. It is utterly still, hidden

and lonesome, nothing but God in his purity reigns there, nothing alien or creaturely, no image or sound have ever reached thus far.

Our Lord spoke of this solitude when he bade the prophet Joel (Osee) speak thus: 'I will lead my own into the wilderness and I will speak to their hearts.' This wilderness is his silent, lonesome Godhead to which he wants to lead all those who are to be taught to respond to his whisper, now and in all eternity. Take your vain and lonely ground, which is filled with weeds and devoid of all goodness, and where the wild beasts of your animal senses and forces reign supreme, into God's solitary, still and free ground.

Then you will contemplate the divine darkness, which by its blinding clearness appears dark to human and even to the angels' understanding, just as the resplendent orb of the sun appears dark to the weak eye; for it is in the nature of all created understanding that, compared with the divine clarity, it is as small as a swallow's eye when compared with the size of the sun and as far as this understanding is merely of the natural order it must be beaten back into unconsciousness so that it can do no more harm.

You should, however, endure your abysmal darkness, devoid and in need of the true light as it is, and leave the deep gulf of divine darkness to be known only to itself, unknown to all creatures and things. This gulf, unaware, unnamed and blessed, inspires more love and sets more souls aflame than all the understanding of the divine Being which can be gained in eternal bliss.

COMMIT THY WAY TO THE LORD
AND TRUST IN HIM

Commit thy way to the Lord and trust in him; and he will do it. And he will bring forth thy justice as the light and thy judgement as the noonday. Be subject to the Lord and pray to him. (Psalm 36, 5.)

Thus speaks the prophet of the Psalm: 'Commit thy way to the Lord, trust in him and he will do it.'

We should always bear these words in mind, because whosoever is in search of the path leading to a pious life will find in them the solution to all his problems: 'Commit thy way to the Lord, trust in him and he will do it.'

Well, children, now I shall talk to you about your spiritual and bodily exercises because just as a good wine must be kept in a good cask, a wholesome and orderly body is the proper foundation for a well-appointed inner ground, for good works and practices.

The practices I am speaking of are watching, fasting and keeping silence. But which is the best way to fast? Those of the sisters who can do it easily without damaging their health should observe the strict rule, although by no means do I insist upon it. But whatever you do, you should take nourishment in the morning of that kind of food which sustains your body—and have but little to eat in the evening, as this benefits both the body and the spirit. You should go to bed in the early evening immediately after Compline, so that you may be all the fresher after midnight and are able to turn to God with more fervour. But should some among you not find sleep in the evening they should not be troubled, but rather think over the things they want to do after Mass.

Above all, learn to preserve your inner peace. After Mass you ought to remain in choir for the duration of a sung Mass and concentrate on the state of your heart and soul; when your head begins to feel heavy and your body is weary, go to a place where you can sit in comfort, so that your body is at ease, either by or on your bed, and there you may turn your mind to your inner being. When the body is overworked and restless it takes its toll in various ways and the result is that you fall into a heavy and leaden sleep.

When you have thus settled down you should consider the verse from the Psalm: *Revela domino viam tuam et spera in eo et ipse faciet*, 'Commit thy way to the Lord, trust in him and he will do it.' What is it, then, that you should commit to our Lord, to whom all things are known and revealed? It means that you should examine yourselves and establish what your own way really is.

The first step towards this aim is taken when you honestly acknowledge your faults, from the bottom of your heart. This is the first condition which all the chosen friends of God must fulfil. You should bewail your faults, whatever they may be, and tell God about your shortcomings as well as about the graces and virtues for which you long; you will then be speaking to your truest and dearest friend to whom you can disclose all your defects and lament your faults because he is the One in whom you can utterly trust. *Et ipse faciet*, and he will do it. Believe only in him! If there were two people who prayed to our Lord, the one entirely trustful, praying for a big thing which seemed impossible to fulfil, and the other only praying for a petty thing yet not trusting our Lord implicitly, it is far more likely that the prayer of the one who prayed for the big thing would be heard. Christ said that all things are possible to the man of faith, and believe me, he was only thinking of that utter trust in God, for the prophet said: 'He will do it' and neither God nor the prophet tell lies. Put your whole trust in him and remember that it is equally impossible to love him too much as it is to trust him too much. Whatever it is you want to say or complain about to me or your teachers or good friends, tell him instead and offer your troubles up to him. *Et ipse faciet*. He prefers to do it if you willingly accept what he sends you and he gives with much more joy when you accept joyfully. If you want to atone for your sins and receive grace, put your whole trust in him and do not imagine that a different sort of life would bring you nearer to him.

This, then, is the way to acquire virtues and to cast out vices. Even when man turns into himself and receives no particular comfort from God, he should concentrate, for the sake of God, on those spiritual exercises to which he is used and which make him most conscious of God's grace, whether they be concerned with our Lord's life, Passion or his wounds.

All this should be accomplished without self-will, so that man can follow God when he wants to draw him into himself; if God should choose to draw him to a higher spiritual level, man should not try to scrutinise his state with the help of his senses, but should simply leave everything to God and tell him to 'do it'. Put your trust in him and when you think that you want either to pray for someone else or for the forgiveness of your sins, put it simply into his charge. *Spera in eo*, he will do it.

Never give way to despondency, for it prevents the good in you from growing. If you notice that God wants to draw you into your inner being, let go of everything, images and all, and obey him. Should you catch sight of something else, disregard it, as you must also reject divine visions; do not attempt to achieve anything with the help of the senses, but should you not be able to follow these directions, commit them to him and 'he will do it'. Towards dawn, sleep may claim you and, children, such a slumber strengthens and purifies your body and mind, your brains are cleared and all next day you will be settled, at peace, and feel the better for your spiritual exercises, which have united you to God. Thus all your activities will be subordinated to God and if carefully planned and motivated by virtue, when actually performed they will be good and holy.

If, however, dear children, you should fall asleep against your will, I shall tell you what to do. A good meditation, even when interrupted by occasional nodding, is much more beneficial than many outward exercises of the senses while one is wide awake. Start again, then, and say: *Sursum corda*—lift up your hearts, and thus return once more to God. Open your inner ground to him and say with the prophet: *Exquisivit te facies mea; faciem tuam requiram*. 'Lord, my face looks for thine, do not turn it away from me.' In the same way turn your inner soul that it may be beheld by God's countenance, and that the indefinable inner being offers itself to God; the things we can define follow suit and submit to him. On the other hand, the indefinable and unknown, as well as the things to which God has given names, are proffered to you that they may be beheld in your inner ground.

It is therefore of great assistance if you are outwardly at peace, when you sit still and keep quiet and also when your body shows no signs of unrest. Dear children, if you are thus tranquil God will give himself and the kingdom to you.

The next verse runs as follows: *Et deducit quasi lumen justitiam tuam*, 'and he brings forth thy justice as the light'. And what, pray, is our justice? None other than that we know ourselves.

St Bernard said: 'The best and the highest knowledge necessary for our approach to God is to know ourselves.'

'He brings forth the justice as the light.' Children, your justice is determined by the behaviour of your holy order, but infinitely more so by your silence. This you should practise at all times and in all places according to your rules. I ask you in the name of God to observe them and to keep away from people, whoever they may be, particularly from such lighthearted people whose minds are not in search of what you hope to attain. You should have no contact with them except an occasional friendly 'Yes' or 'No'. If they want to misinterpret your behaviour, let them do so, unless they are prepared to follow you on your way to God. I also ask of you that you do not secretly admit someone from the world whose character you do not know; altogether I would advise you to keep clear of men and women if you want to avoid being misled. There is so much that you can listen to or read that it ought to suffice. Keep to yourselves, do not turn to people who use big words, but remain within your inner being.

The verse continues: *et judicium tuum tamquam meridiem*, 'and thy judgement shall be as the noonday'. What is this judgement of yours that should be so bright? It is the sentence you pass on yourselves. St Paul said: 'If we condemn ourselves we shall not be condemned.' Whenever man realises how lofty, pure and noble he was before he was born and how low and crude he has become since, he must needs condemn himself and acknowledge his inferiority; this knowledge results in such an unutterable self-condemnation that, if it were possible, he would be willing to obliterate himself. As soon, however, as man has passed censure on himself, his 'judgement is as bright as the noonday.'

When in summer the sun stands at its zenith, its rays are so hot that, if they were not tempered by the clouds, they would burn the grass and all the plants. God must deal in the same way with people who utterly condemn themselves; if it were not for the sanctifying grace of which he allows them to have an occasional glimpse, and which tempers the terrible judgement and self-obliteration to which they subject themselves, they could not endure its intensity. There was a man who had such an experience. He was exposed to such a fire of self-condemnation that he thought he would burst into

flames and be reduced to nothing so that God had
to soothe him.

The verse goes on to say: *Subditus esto domino et
ora eum,* 'be subject to the Lord and pray to him.'
You should understand this prayer in the following
way: you should subject yourselves to God in all
humility and the core of your soul should be in such
a state of discernment and contemplation of his
Spirit that you, with all your faults, your nothingness, your virtues and good works, should prostrate
yourselves outside the gates of Paradise, from whence
God's mercy streams forth in an eternal flow of love
and goodness. This subjection should emanate from
your mind and your spiritual discernment and it is of
an entirely different order than are your everyday
vigils and devotional readings. These two kinds of
devotion are as different from each other as running
is from sitting still.

Dear children, turn your whole attention and
fervour to your inner ground and do not tie yourselves to the practices of the senses. Go boldly
forward into your inner being and from there let
all your works come forth, whether they be of the
high realm of the mind or for the glory of the
sublime Passion of our Lord Jesus Christ.

Make it your particular act of devotion to sink
into the five glorious signs of God's love—his
wounds.

Take your strong desires and bury them in the
sacred wound of his left foot, your vicious temper
into that of the right foot, put your self-will into the
wound of the left hand and then, using the whole
strength of your senses, approach and sink your
mind into the wound of the right hand, so that he

may adjust and govern your inner being with his divine strength. Finally, with all your power of love, seek refuge in his divine loving heart which remains open to receive you, to unite you with him, to draw away your love from everything impure and irrelevant and, by the merit of his five sacred wounds and bitter Passion, to absorb you, body and mind.

All this you must practise with much fervour and let us pray to God that he accomplishes it within you to his greater glory. Amen.